Make Your Own
Egyptian Jewelry

Custom Fitted Ancient Egyptian Styled Jewelry
Made Easy Enough for Beginners

Dawna Flowers

Make Your Own Egyptian Jewelry was written by Dawna Flowers
Published by Amazon, for Under the Moon Publishing, 2019.

ISBN: 9781700153968

INTRODUCTION

Ancient Egyptian Jewelry

Egyptian collar necklaces, also called *gorgets*, were used by the Ancient Egyptians in even their earliest periods. The collar necklace has long since been one of the prevalent trademark icons of the Ancient Egyptian culture. Kohl painted eyes, arm braces, elaborate belts, and headdress share the limelight with the collar necklace in Egypt's pictorial history, but the gorget remains a constant when all others come and go.

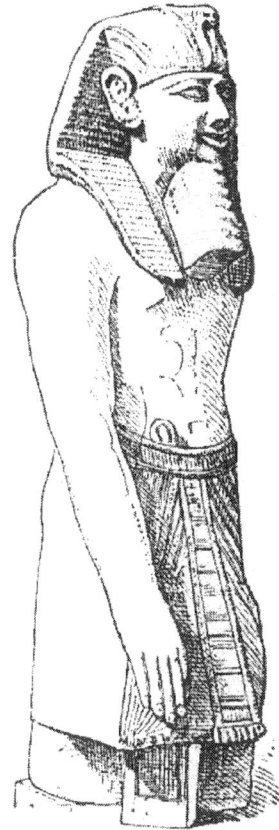

Armbands, anklets, and bracelets also played a very prominent role in Ancient Egyptian dress, and can bee seen in thousands of depictions throughout Egypt. Often, these pieces were very broad, but the Egyptians did wear dainty jewelry too, as their styles varied with each generation.

While the gorget and braces essentially remain the same throughout Egyptian history, the belt underwent constant changes. There are hundreds of various belt styles that range from beaded - to fabric - to pure metal designs, depending on the period and the popular artisans.

Jewelry played a very important part in Ancient artworks and writings. Regardless if the ancient depictions were elaborate statues, or simple caricatures, the collar necklace was a staple ornament in almost all Ancient Egyptian art. While diadems and headdresses were usually reserved for royalty, priest, priestess, Gods and Goddesses, the braces and gorgets were not. Almost anyone in good standing was depicted as adorning a gorget. Cats, which were believed to embody the essence of the Goddess Bast, were also adorned with these beautiful necklaces. Everyone from the Gods, to simple workers were seen wearing these trademark pieces, even the deceased.

Jewelry takes on various artistic styles as dynasties changed hands, but the same basic designs are seen throughout Egypt's history. It is the traditional and constant designs that I have set out to recreate in my own Egyptian inspired jewelry.

When I began playing a live action role-playing game called *Amtgard*, I knew immediately that I wanted my persona to be Ancient Egyptian. A strong interest in the Egyptian culture has held a grip on me since I was a small child, and continues to remain an obsession of mine. When I began compiling my first costume for Amtgard, I purchased a necklace off eBay. The necklace was imported from Egypt and had been produced by local artisans. The necklace was cheap in price, and yet, it looked beautiful; however, it was not exactly the colors I wanted, so I set out to make one of my own, in my own preferred colors.

I used the necklace I had bought as a guideline to make my own, and it worked out fairly well. When I completed my first handmade necklace, I put it on with my garb, and I realized that I was missing something. Accessories!

So, I set out to make earrings, armbands, anklets, and bracelets. After several days of tinkering with different designs, I had completed my task and was very pleased. Once again, I put on my Egyptian jewelry and stood in front of the mirror. I was still missing something. A belt! I then set out to make myself a belt, and when I was finished, I realized that my garb was finally complete as I stood in front of the mirror. I have gone on and since created headdresses, diadems, headbands, hairpins, and hundreds of pieces of various jewelry, but I've since realized that the basic Egyptian garb needs only to consist of the necklaces, braces, and the belt. These pieces are essential to creating beautiful Egyptian garb, and are practical enough to wear weekly. And so, with that epiphany, and dozens of Egyptian sets later, I have created the following book for others, so that I may share my insights and thoughts about Ancient Egyptian inspired jewelry with others, and give you, my dear reader, the knowledge to create your own Egyptian treasures.

Modern Techniques

The patterns in this book will create a full set of Egyptian garb to be worn, not just admired. The jewelry is functional, and the pieces I have created for myself are worn often. I have a favorite set, which I wear every Sunday, and it has held up exceptionally well.

The patterns in this book consist primarily of bars full of beads, unlike the traditional strand of beads that interconnect. With each piece of jewelry, (except for the earrings) you will have a few strands that connect the bars together, while the bars themselves create the bulk of the designs. This technique serves several purposes. Working with bars, instead of one single strand is much easier. If you mess up, it's not that big of a deal and you won't have to start the entire piece over. Another benefit of bars is that - in the event that a piece of jewelry breaks, it doesn't completely fall apart. Repairs to this type of jewelry are incredibly simple to perform.

Many archeological pieces found in Egypt were actually constructed with similar bars, making this jewelry very similar to the way that certain pieces were created by ancient artisans of Egypt. Although, the Egyptians were known to create pieces using a wide variety of techniques, and this technique is only one of many.

When creating your own jewelry from the patterns in this book, I encourage you to create your own patterns as you go, to make an even more personalized set. Where I have small beads, you can replace them with larger beads if you would like, simply by changing the number of beads on each bar, which you will learn more about in just a moment.

Creating your own pattern is very easy and you only have to design a couple of bars at a time. For example, as you will see, the first row of the necklace is comprised of one bar that is repeated over and over. The second row of the necklace is just two bars that are repeated over and over. The third row only has four bars that are repeated. If you can design a few bars at a time, you will be able to create your own original pattern with a variety of your favorite beads. Typically, it will take me several days, or several weeks to create a full set of garb, which includes a necklace, belt, and a pair each of armbands, bracelets, anklets, and earrings. I usually work on the set for about two to six hours a day, when time permits. If this is your first time at making a set, it may take you a little longer until you get the hang of it. The fun thing about these sets are when you have made one, it is exceptionally easy to create a second set completely on your own, without any instruction. You can let your creative juices flow and design a beautiful set all on your own.

Supplies & Tools

Before you begin your beading project, you will want to make sure you have accumulated all of the tools and supplies that you will need to finish your project without interruption. In this section, you will find the supplies and tools needed for this particular project, however, if your own pattern differs from the one here, you will need to make the adjustments to fit your own project.

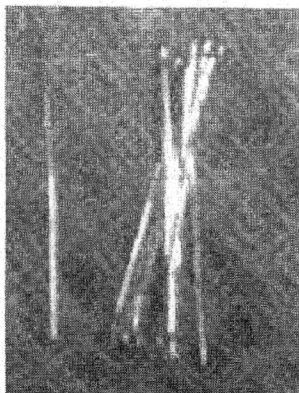

During the course of producing your Egyptian jewelry, you will be placing beads onto the eye pins, and then you will be looping the tip of the pin, so that the pin will look like the illustration below, to the right. I would recommend practicing making the loops before starting the project. You will want to make a loop that is as closed as possible, to ensure that the beading thread does not slip out of the loop. In addition, you will want to make sure that the loop you make is facing the same direction as the one already pre-made.

2" Pins
We will be using two types of pins: The eye pin, and the head pin

2" Eye Pin   **2" Head Pin**   **Looped Eye Pin**

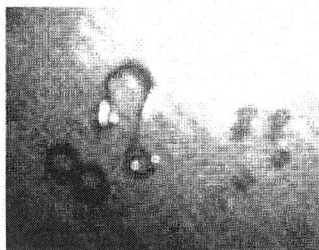

Clasps
You will also need 2 pairs of clasps: One for the belt, and one for the necklace. The clasps you use are, of course, up to you, but the clasps I prefer are the hook and eye clasps. Typically, they come in two per package.

Beads

For this learning project, we will be using a variety of beads in different sizes and colors. The colors you prefer may differ from those used in these instructions. As long as the predominately-used beads are similar in size to the pattern, you should have no problems. The jewelry I will be instructing you to make is custom fitted for me, and I will be instructing you along the way, so you will be able to make a custom fitted set for yourself.

The beads that we will be using the most are detailed for you below.
NOTE: The white denotes gold beads, while the grey denotes red beads.

O ● The gold beads are 4mm. The red beads are 6/0. (I will refer to these sizes as SMALL)

O ● Both Red and Gold Sizes: 6mm (I will refer to this size as MEDIUM)

♦ These beads are a darker red, and are slightly larger than the small red and gold beads seen above. These particular beads came within a red/orange assortment pack called Asian Spice, so I do not have a size for them. To match the size for your own pattern, simply pick a bead that is slightly larger than the 6/0, but not as large as the 6mm, and it should work just fine. (I will refer to this bead as SMALL SPICE.)

There are other larger beads used in this pattern that you will be using to create accent areas within the necklace and belt. All of the red beads below are ones that came within the Asian Spice Assortment pack and all have a darker red, ruby look to them. Again, because these beads were included within an assortment pack, I do not have sizes for them. I encourage you to shop your local bead store to find styles that you prefer and accommodate the pattern to your own beads. As long as your accent beads are less than an inch long, you should be able to successfully use them with these instructions. I recommend though, that you choose beads that are ½ inch wide or less, and less than an inch long in length. The gold (white) bead shown on the left is a standard sized bugle (spaghetti) bead.

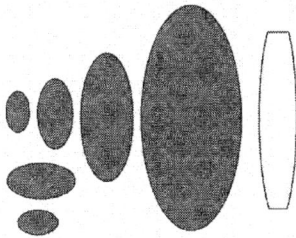

Crimp Beads

Crimp Beads are small gold, silver, or brass colored metal beads that one places on the end of a cord or wire and clamps it in place with pliers or a crimping tool. So, why crimp beads and not just knots? Crimp beads will dig into the cord or wire, creating a very stable anchor to hold the strand together, and rarely come apart, unless under extreme pressure.

Beading Cord and Wire

The wire or cord you use is of your choosing; however, because this is going to be a heavy project, I would strongly suggest that you use high quality, durable materials. I prefer Soft Flex© Medium sized Beading Wire for the belt and necklace; however, for the bracelets, anklets, and armbands, I prefer to use 1mm clear Stretch Magic© beading cord.

Pliers

For this project, you will need curling pliers to curl the tip of the eye pins. This is the most important tool when creating these Egyptian styled designs, as you will need to loop many, many eye pins. These pliers are similar to needle nosed pliers, except the tips of these pliers have rounded, barrel looking noses that come to a point, as shown in the picture.

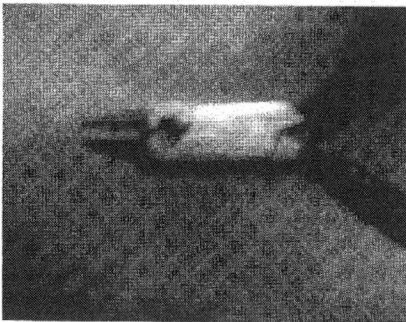

Optional Tools & Accessories

Bead Boxes

When starting a project, I always begin by organizing my beads into one box. I have another box in which I keep my tools, so when I'm working on a project I only have two containers that I work from: one for beads, and another for tools. This makes the projects easy to transport and very portable. They also keep the beads from spilling out, and it keeps them separated. These boxes can be purchased for less than two dollars, so they are indeed a wise investment.

Other Pliers

During my beading project, I primarily use the curling pliers, as previously seen; however, other tools may also come in handy. For example, to crimp the crimp beads, you may wish to obtain crimping pliers. You will be able to crimp the crimp beads with the curling pliers, but crimping pliers will work slightly better. Needle nose pliers may come in handy if you have to make corrections, as they will allow you to grip much better than other pliers will. Depending on which type of wire you use, you may want to invest in a pair of wire cutters, although scissors can perform just as good, providing they are very sharp. Illustrated in the picture, from left to right are: Needle Nosed Gripping Pliers, Crimping Pliers, Wire Cutters, and Rounded Curling Pliers.

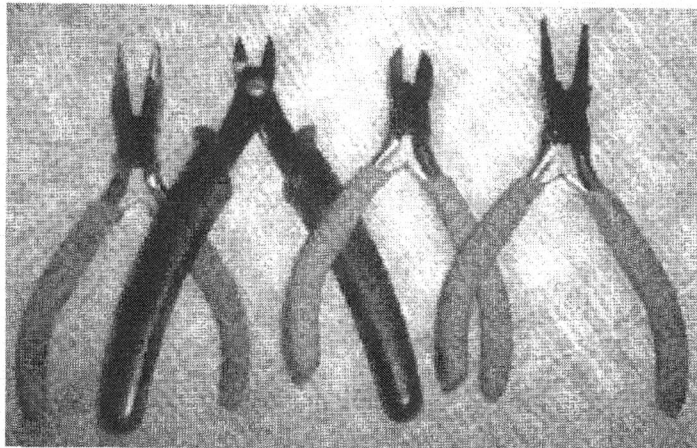

EGYPTIAN COLLAR
NECKLACE

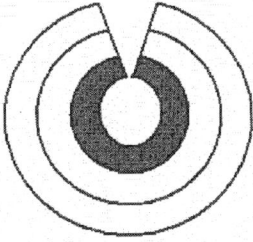

Egyptian Collar Necklace
First Row

Take note of the picture in the corner above. You will see similar pictures through out this book. These highlighted areas indicate which piece of jewelry and more specifically, which part of the jewelry project we are discussing. These will provide you with easy referencing when you are flipping through pages looking for a particular spot. Now, let's begin creating the first row of our necklace!

To begin your necklace, gather your wire, three crimp beads, and your crimping tool (or pliers). Measure around your neck with the wire to see how long you want your necklace to be. You can make the necklace almost a choker, or make it a little longer, it's up to you. I would recommend using a length that would be a little bit longer than a choker. If you make the necklace fit too snug around your neck, it may not lay flat as you wear it, so a good rule of thumb is to measure around the base of your neck and add about two or three inches to get the length. The wire will also need to be three or four additional inches longer than you want the necklace to be. This will allow you additional wire to add the clasps, and to make adjustments if needed throughout your project.

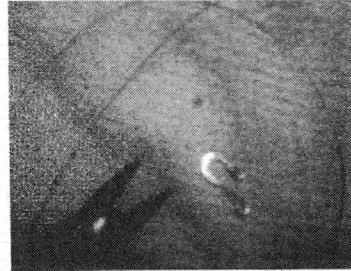

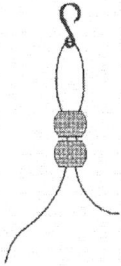

Once you have your materials ready, the first thing you will need to do is attach a clasp to one end of the wire. Do this by threading two crimp beads on first, then add the clasp, slide the other end of the thread through the crimp bead so that you've made a loop, as shown in the picture. Next, slide the crimp bead close to the clasp, and then crimp the beads using your pliers. Cut off the excess wire once you are done. Now, you will need to put the wire aside for a moment.

We will now prepare the beaded bars. For this, you will need eye pins, and the rounded needle nosed pliers, and of course, your small beads. The pattern that I have chosen for the first row of bars is: 4 red, 1 gold, 1 red, 1gold, 1 small spice, 1 gold, 1 red, 1 gold, 4 red, as shown in the illustrations on the side. You may also refer to the cover of this book for color references. When you have placed the beads on the bar, you will need to create a small loop at the top of the bar that will hold the beads in place. This loop will also serve as a means of lacing the bars together later on. When you make your loop, make sure that the loop is aligned with the pre-existing loop. If your loops face a different direction, this will cause problems when you lace your bars together. Make sure to make your loops as closed as possible. Leaving small gaps in your loops will allow your wire to slip out and cause your bars to fall off the necklace.

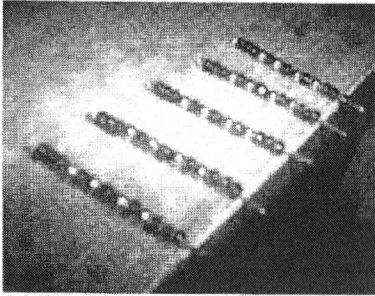

Obviously, you can bead the bars individually and loop them one at a time, as you go. Personally, I like to bead a bunch of bars, then loop them all later. I place the beads on the bars, and then lay the bars on the edge of a table. Once I have a bunch of bars ready to be looped, I begin looping. This helps break the monotony of beading and looping repeatedly.

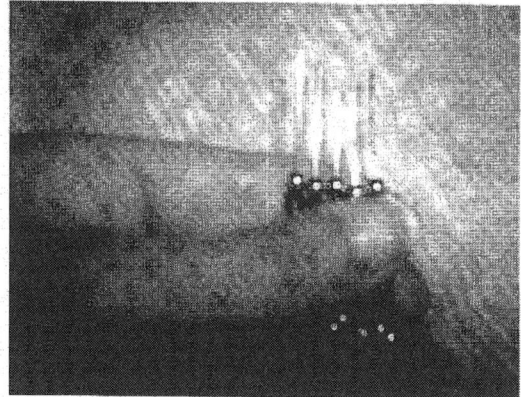

Once you get the hang of beading the bars individually, you can try doing several at a time by holding several bars in your hands at once and beading them with your other hand.

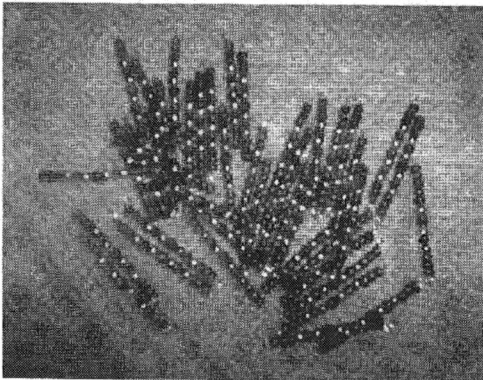

Once you have around 50 bars completed, collect the wire (with the already attached clasp) and we will start lacing the bars together. Start by adding one small gold bead, and now add your first bar. Then, add a large gold bead, another bar, and repeat. Be sure to lace all the bars together so that the loops are facing the same direction. The picture below illustrates four bars facing the same direction, with one on the left that is not. If you accidentally place a bar on wrong, don't worry, it's not too big of a deal. You can fix it later without having to unlace the whole strand. Just use your pliers to open the loop, take the bar out, turn the bar around, and close the loop with your pliers.

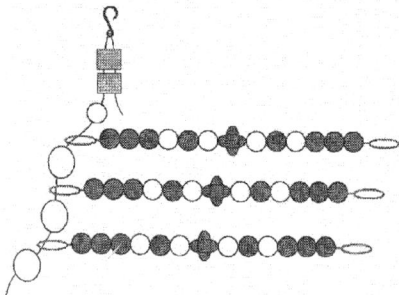

The picture here illustrates how you should lace the bars together. Your row pattern will be: bar, medium gold bead, bar, medium gold bead, bar, and so forth. Lace all of the bars onto the wire and test it occasionally to see if the length is looking good.

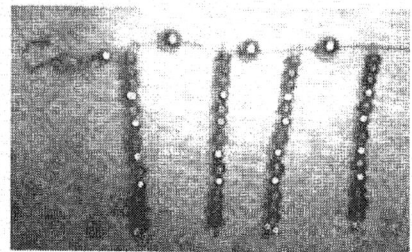

Because I am a small person, with a small neck and shoulder area, I have only used around fifty bars for the first row. The average person will probably need between 55-65 bars for the first row. The quantity of bars you will need also greatly depends on the size of the spacer beads. If you use smaller beads between the bars, you will need more bars. If you use larger beads between the bars, then you will need fewer bars to complete your desired length.

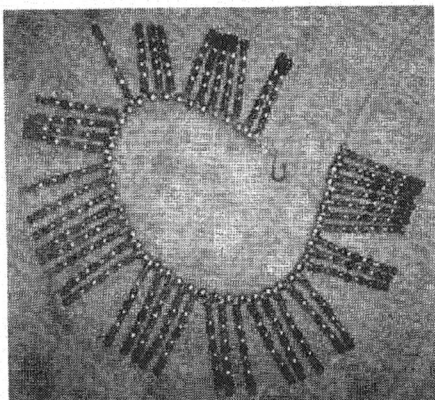

Once you have the strand at the length that you like, you are almost ready to add the other clasp. Once you have placed your last bar on the strand, add one small gold bead, then add two crimp beads, and then slide on your clasp. Loop the loose end of the thread through the two crimp beads (just like you did for the first clasp). Before you crimp your beads, make sure that the strand is not too tight, and not too loose. You will want to leave about ¼ of an inch of slack on the strand so that the bars can move with you while you are wearing it. If your strand is too tight, you will risk breaking beads, or it will force the crimp beads to fly off under pressure. If your strand is too loose, then gaps will be visible while you wear it.

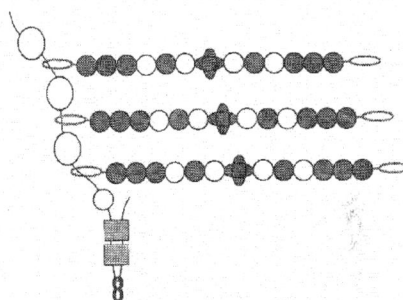

Your first completed row should look similar to the illustration below. Don't worry if your bars don't seem to hang evenly, and some seem to want to hang closer together than others. They will come together nicely when you have laced together the second row.

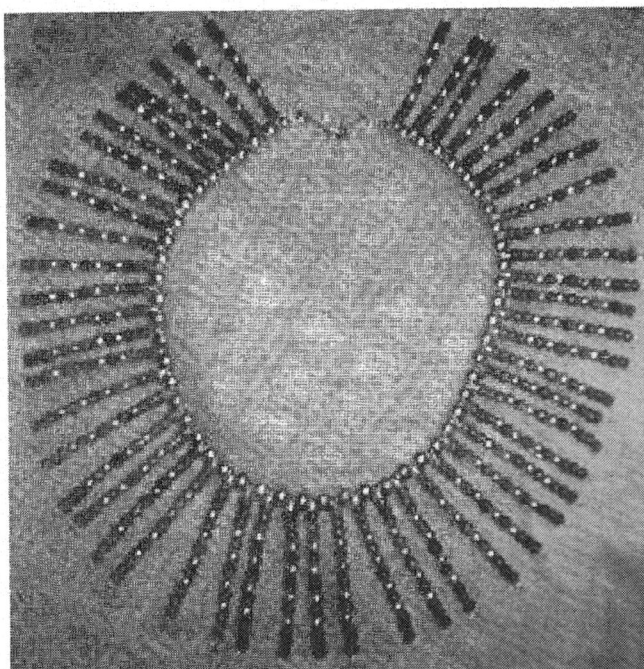

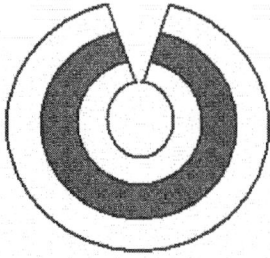

Egyptian Collar Necklace
Second Row

Now you are ready to proceed with creating the second row. By now, you have probably gotten the hang of creating the bars and are a little more confident, and even a little quicker. By the time you finish this project you will be spitting out bars quicker than you thought possible!

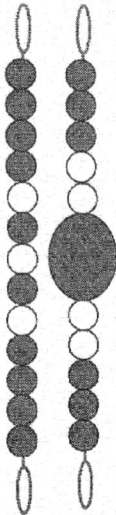

For the second row, you will be creating two separate groups of bars with different patterns. Count the bars that you used in making the first row, and make the same amount of bars for each pattern. For example, if you used 50 bars in the first row, then you will need to make 50 bars of the first pattern, and 50 bars of the second pattern, for a total of 100 new bars to create the second row.

When you have your bars completed, you are now ready to connect them to the first row. You will be alternating the bars as you lace them, as shown in the picture to the right.

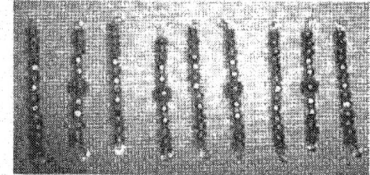

Begin the second row by deciding how much wire you will need. Measure the first row, then double it, and this should give you more than enough wire. Now, attach two crimp beads to the end of the wire and crimp them down tight. Add one small gold bead, and then lace the wire through the first bar of the top row. Add the first bar from the second row, add a small gold bead, and then add the second bar of the second row, one small gold bead. Now lace it through the bottom of the second bar of the first row. Sounds complicated, I know, but it's much easier than it sounds, as you can see from the picture. It may be frustrating at first, and you may mess up several times, but the trick is to get yourself into a groove. I personally create small chants to hum quietly to myself as I lace them along to help get into a groove.

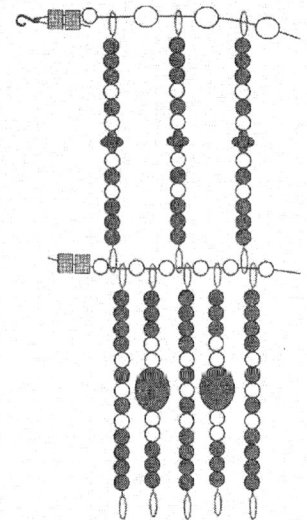

20

For example, for connecting the second row, I would silently chant in my mind something like this: "Bead – Top bar – Bottom bar – Bead – Other bottom bar..."then start the chant over and repeat until the second row is completely attached.

As you go along, you may notice some bars that are bent, simply straighten them out with your fingers before lacing them. When you have added all the bars, make sure that the last bar of the second row joins up with the last bar in the first row, as show in the picture. This may require you to discard a bar or two, or to create an additional bar or two. After you have placed the very last bar on the second row, you can now add one small gold bead and two crimp beads to the wire. Leave about two inches of slack along the wire (you will adjust this later.) Now add a third crimp bead to the very end of the wire and crimp it in place (remember to leave the slack.)

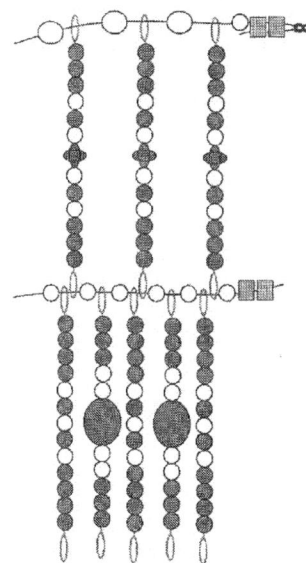

When you are completely done with the second row, you should notice that your collar necklace is coming along nicely, and it should look similar to the photo below.

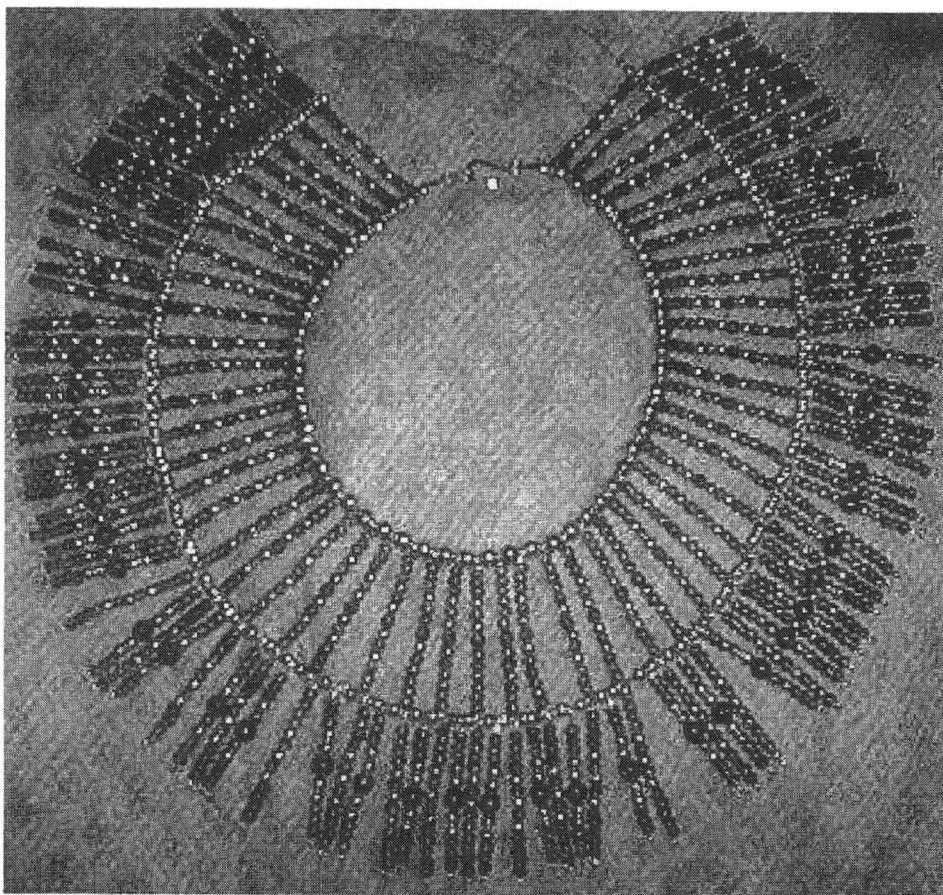

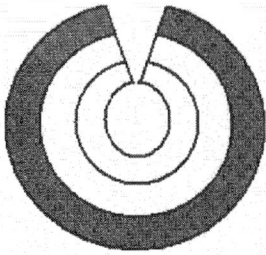

Egyptian Collar Necklace
Third Row

Now you are ready to proceed with creating the third and final row to your necklace. Unfortunately, to create a fully customized necklace, with proportionally placed accent areas, it will take a small bit of math. Don't panic! It's not too difficult and a pen and paper are all you will need. I promise, you will not need a complicated graphing calculator to finish this project!

The first thing you will need to do is count how many bars you used in the second row. This number count will be the same amount of bars that you will need for the third row. Now, you need to decide how many accent bars you want on your third row. For this pattern, I have decided to have two different accent bars, and one main bar. Since I have slightly over 100 bars on my second row, I have decided that I would like my accent bars to be spaced ten bars apart. I have also alternated my accent bars. Because I have 103 bars to be placed on the third row, I have decided to have 9 accent bars instead of ten, which means that I will have a few uneven spaces on the back of the necklace. This will not be a problem, and will look just fine. Rarely will you have the exact number of bars needed to create a perfectly spaced necklace when you are designing a custom fit piece. If you will look at the completed necklace picture on the next page, you will see that it appears proportional regardless, so don't sweat it too much.

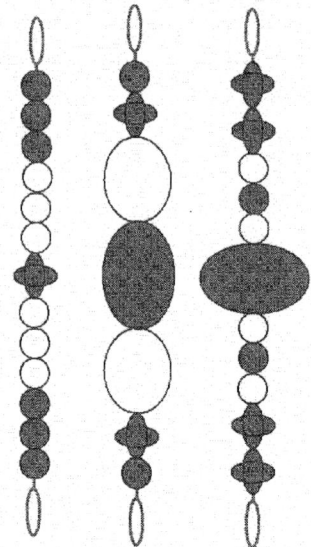

The easiest way to come up with a decent space between the accent bars is to take the total number of bars needed for the second row and divide it by ten. If you find that ten spaces just doesn't work for you, then you can experiment with blank bars by lying them in place without threading them. In other necklaces, I have spaced the highlight bars anywhere from three to fifteen spaces apart. It really depends on how big the beads are on the highlight bars, how many of them you have, and what design you are trying to achieve. Just tinker around with it until you come up with an equation that works for your necklace. I find that the bigger the highlight beads are, the farther apart you will want to place them; otherwise, it will draw attention to the individual beads, instead of the necklace as a whole. If you find that you're just

not up for the math, then you can also alternate two patterns, like we did for the second row. You could even alternate three, or even four different bar patterns.

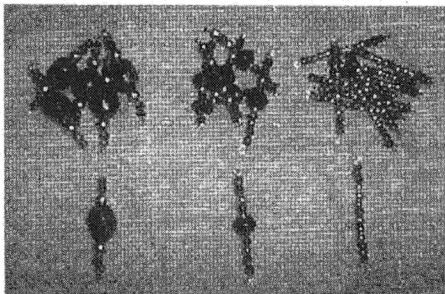

I have decided to use a simple bar, and two highlight bars as illustrated in the pattern above. I used a total of 93 simple bars, four small highlight bars, and five larger highlight bars, but the number you use will vary, depending on the length of your necklace.

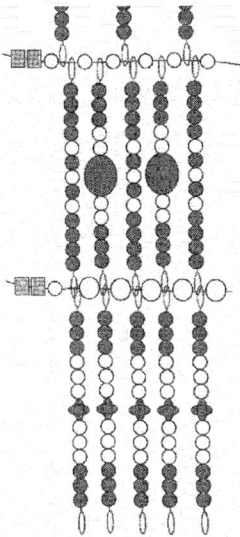

The beads that I chose to use on this necklace are irregular shaped, but you may use whatever shape you would like. Just make sure the beads will fit onto the eye pins with room left over to add at least one small bead on top and one small bead on the bottom, and you then have room left over to curl the loop at the top.

When you have decided on your choice of beads, and have established how many accent bars you want, you are ready to start putting together the bars. Once you have all of the bars completed, you will need to measure how much wire you need by either doubling the amount you used for the second row, or laying the necklace out and estimating. (Don't' estimate too short or you will have to start the row over with a longer wire!)

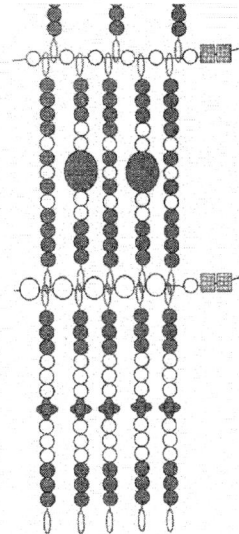

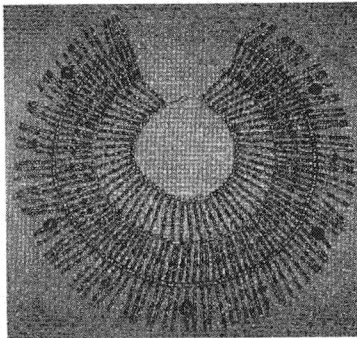

Place two crimp beads onto the end of the wire and crimp them into place. Now, add one small gold bead, lace the top of the first bar of the third row through the bottom of the first bar of the second row, then add a medium gold bead, and repeat. You will be lacing the third row onto the second, in a similar manner that you attached the second row to the first row.

Once you have all of the bars added, make sure that the last bar lines up with the last bar of the second row, the same as you did before. Add one small gold bead to the wire and then add two crimp beads. Leave a couple of inches of slack, then add a third crimp bead to the very end of the wire and clamp into place.

Now you are ready to lace together the very bottom of the necklace. Again, measure how much string you will need by laying the necklace out and measuring, or by doubling the length of string you used for the previous row. Add two crimp beads to the end of the string and crimp them down. Now add a small gold bead, then lace the string through the bottom of the first bar. Now add one medium gold bead, then a small gold bead, and lace it through the second bar, and continue until you have finished lacing the entire row.

Your almost done! Now, lay the necklace out flat. Remember the slack we left on each row? And, the extra un-crimped crimp beads? We are almost ready to address the slack and extra crimp beads.

Start with the strand on the strand connecting the first row to the second row of bars, and tighten it until you only have about ¼ of an inch of slack. Make sure that it doesn't bunch up. The necklace should remain flat. Crimp the beads in place and cut off the excess string.

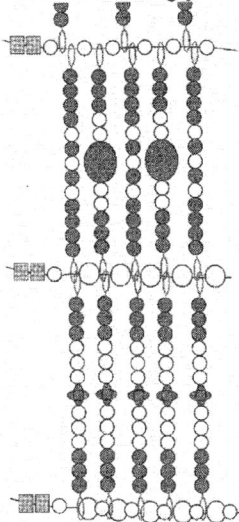

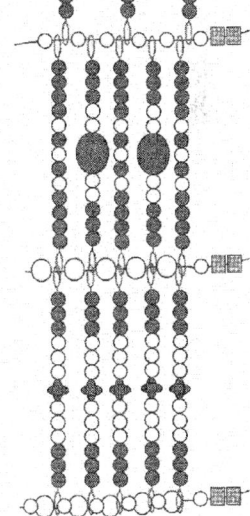

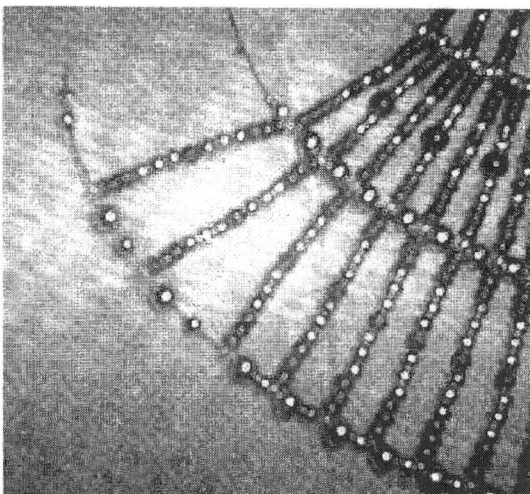

Now do the same for the other rows below, going from the top to the bottom, making sure that each time you tighten a row that the necklace remains flat, and doesn't bunch up. If it bunches up, you have tightened it too much and the necklace will not lie correctly as you wear it. You may also have someone model the necklace for you as you adjust the tightening to get it perfect. When you are done, it should look similar to the picture below.

As an after thought, I have replaced the first and last bars on each row with bars containing only gold beads. This gives the necklace a little more definition, but is not something you have to do. (You can look at the cover art to see how this looks.) If you decide that this is something you would like to do, you don't have to restring all of the rows. You can easily take the bars off using your pliers by opening the loops and taking them out. Put the new bars in place and tighten the loops with your pliers, and your done!

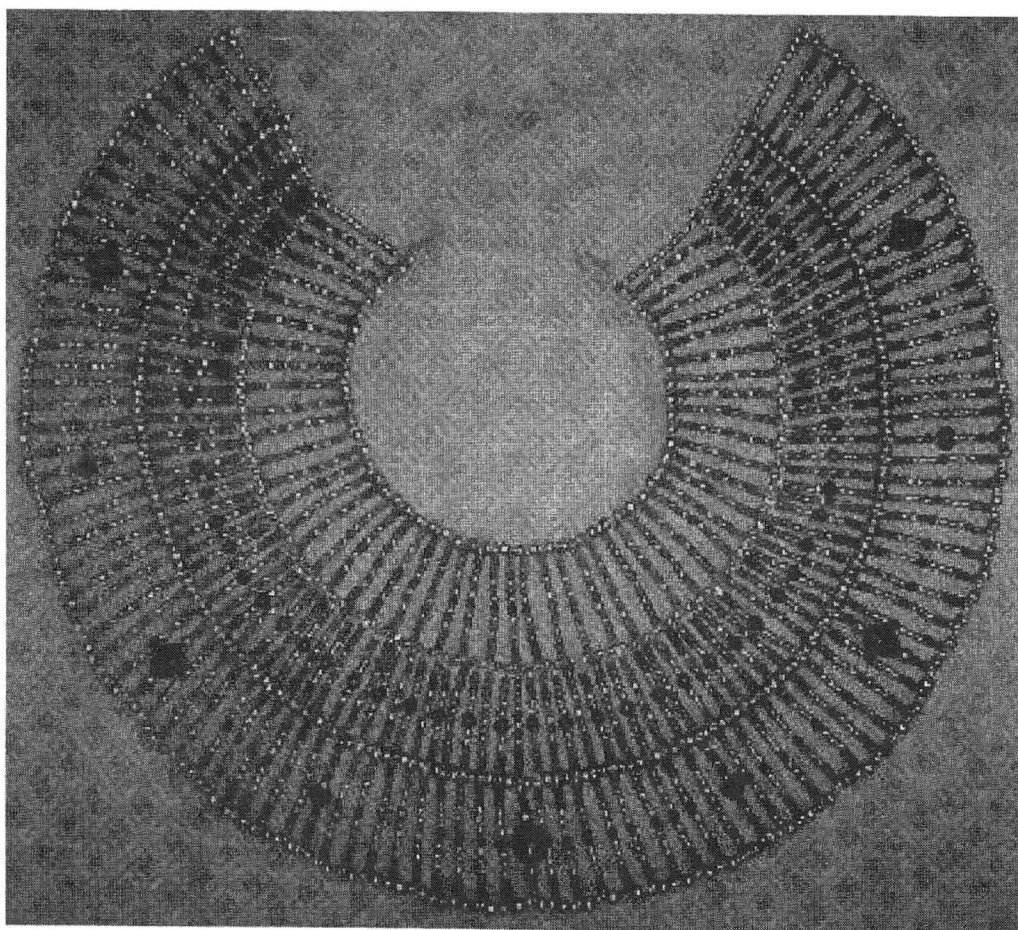

EGYPTIAN STYLED
BELT

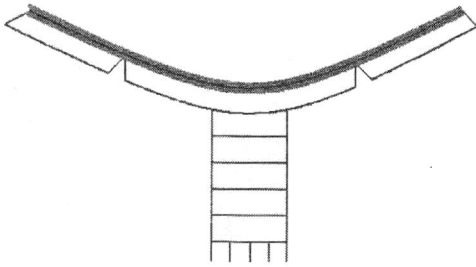

Egyptian Belt
Top Row

Now we will begin the Egyptian Beaded Belt. By now, you should be familiar with making the beaded bars, and lacing them together, so the belt should be easier for you. The only tedious aspect of creating the belt is figuring out where the segments will end, and another begins, as you will want your segments to be as evenly spaced as possible. There will be three segments along the top, consisting of two side segments, and one middle segment.

First, you will need to decide how much wire you will need for the top of the belt. To do this, wrap the wire around you to get an estimate. Leave three or four inches of slack room to be on the safe side. You will need to decide where you want your belt to hang, either high - from the middle of your stomach, or low – from your hips. I prefer a happy medium, not too high on my stomach, and not too low on my hips. Once you have decided on the length, you can add the clasp and fix it in place with the crimp beads, the same way you did with the necklace. Set the wire aside for now, and begin work on the beaded bars.

For the bars, I have used four different bar patterns. I only used two large highlight bars (which will be placed on the sides of the belt later on). I have also used two predominately-gold bars for the first and last bars of the belt. You will only need two each of these bars, which are illustrated in the pattern to the left. The two large oval beaded bars should be made with a flat pin, because you will not be lacing the bottom of it, instead it will dangle.

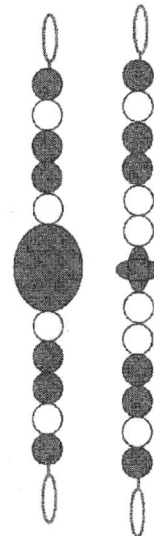

The other bars will make up the bulk of the belt and promote the main pattern. These will consist of two bar patterns, illustrated on the right. The quantity of these main bars you will need will depend entirely on how long your belt is, and is something you will have to figure up as you go, to ensure that you get a perfect fit.

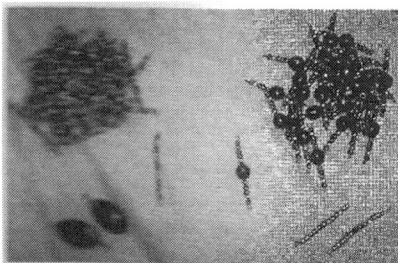

Because I am a small person, wearing pants sized 4 or 5 (depending on the brand) I will only be using around 86 bars for the belt. Two of these bars will be the predominately gold bars seen above. The other highlight bars (the large oval ones seen above) should not enter the equation, as they will be placed between two spacer beads and will not affect the number of bars that you use to create the belt. That leaves me needing 84 bars to create the belt. Because I will be using one of the main bars as a small accent bar, I want fewer of those, since I will placing them as every third bar. I will need approximately 28 of the accent bars, while I will need 56 of the plainer bars. When you have a bunch of bars completed, gather up your wire and add one small gold bead, one of the predominately gold bars, two small gold beads, your first patterned bar, two small gold beads, an accent bar, and continue on until you have reached your desired length. You can use the illustrations below to help guide you.

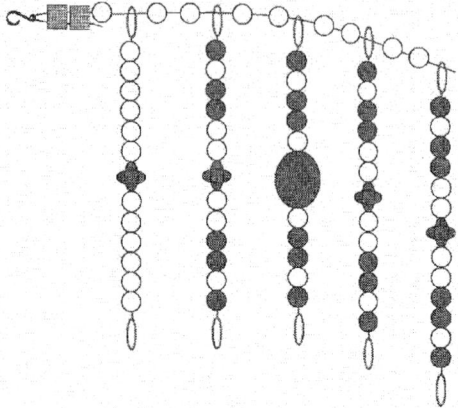

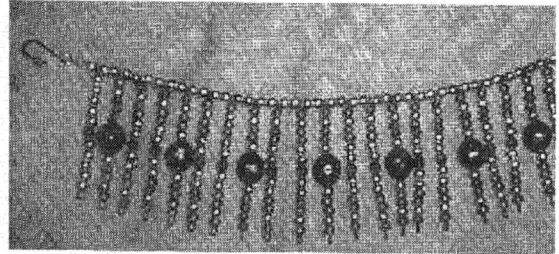

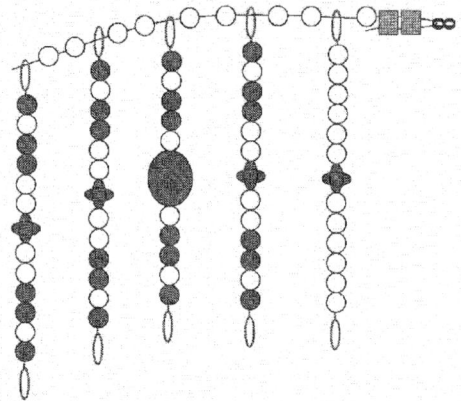

When you have the first row of bars added to the wire, and you have established your desired length, you can then add your last predominately-gold bar, one gold bead, and then two crimp beads. Now attach your clasp by lacing it through the crimp beads and clamping them down. You will want to leave about ¼ of an inch slack so that the strand will not break under pressure as you move.

Once you have the clasp attached, you can put the belt on, and while wearing it, figure out where the sides will be. Make sure that the side segments are even; for example, on my belt, I have 21 bars on each of my side segments. Bear in mind that the side segments will be smaller than the larger middle segment. When you have established where the sides are, you can them place the two large oval accent bars between two of the small gold spacer beads. Do this by opening the top loops with your pliers and attaching them to the strand, then closing the loops.

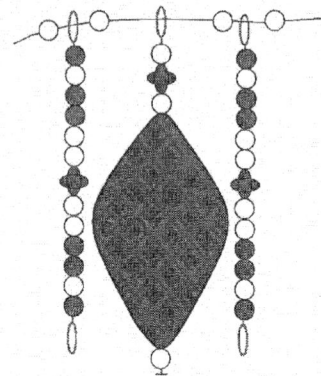

When you are finished with the first row of your belt, it should appear to look similar to the picture below.

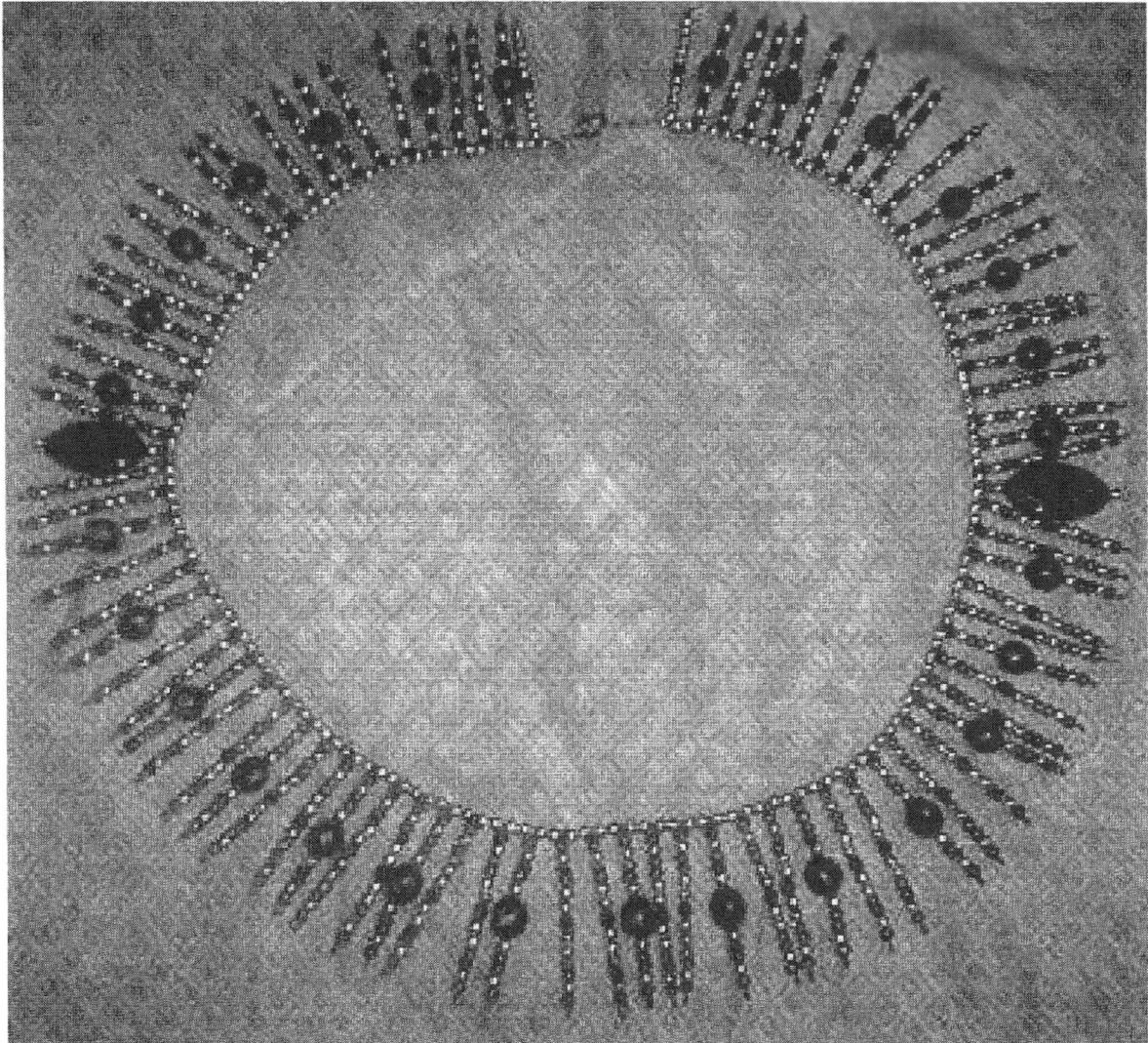

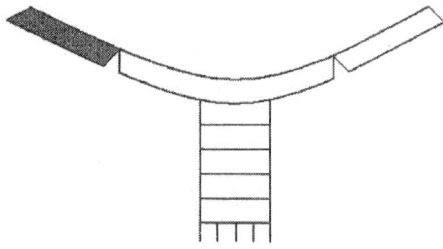

Egyptian Belt
Side Segments

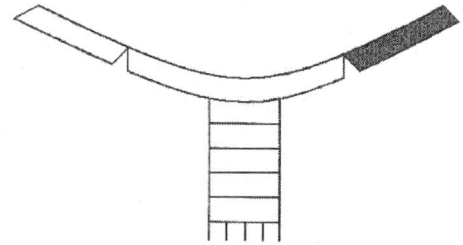

The belt will need to be separated into three segments so that it will lay nicely while you wear it. The ends of the segments should lie at your sides, where you have previously placed the large dangling bars. If we were to make the belt in just one segment, there would be no 'give' room as you move around, and the belt would have to be positioned very high on your stomach. By dividing the belt into three segments, this allows the belt to be placed anywhere along your stomach or hip and will move freely with you.

Now we will finish the side segments. Measure the side segments and cut one piece of wire for each side, leaving a little room for slack. Crimp two beads onto the ends of each wire, add one gold bead, and begin lacing together the bars, with two gold beads between each bar.

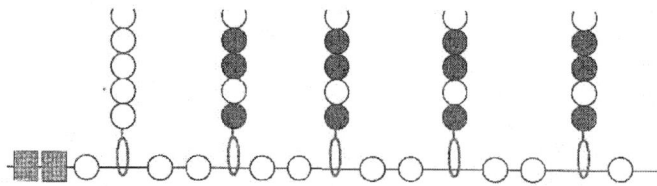

When you have reached the end of the segment and have laced your last bar, add one small gold bead, and two crimp beads. Tighten the segment up until you have less than ¼ of an inch in slack, and crimp down the two crimp beads, then cut off the excess wire. Repeat the process for the other segment.

When you are finished with both segments, your belt should look similar to the illustration below.

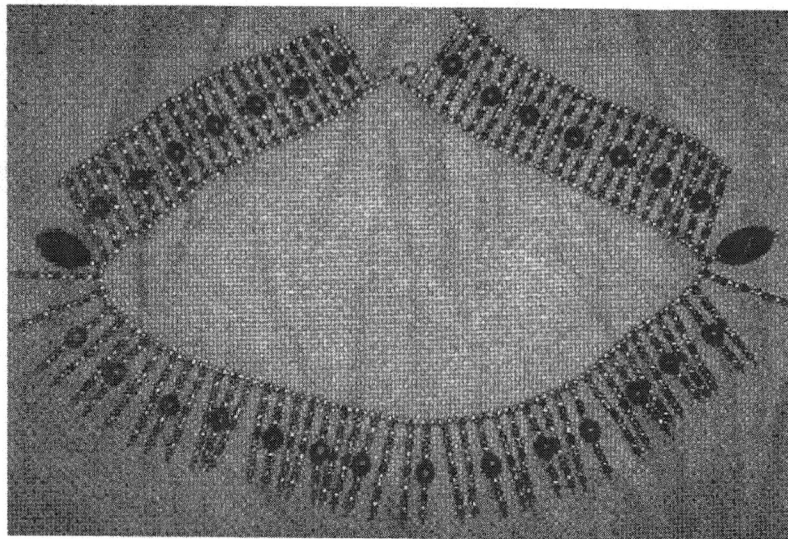

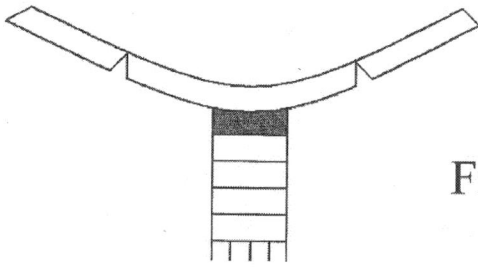

Egyptian Belt
First Hanging Row

Before we can complete the middle segment, we must first prepare the bars for the first hanging row. You will first need to decide how wide you would like the hanging centerpiece to be. I have decided on making mine 17 bars wide. Two of these bars (one on each side) will be plain gold beaded bars. If you are a large person, you may want the centerpiece to be larger, around twenty bars wide.

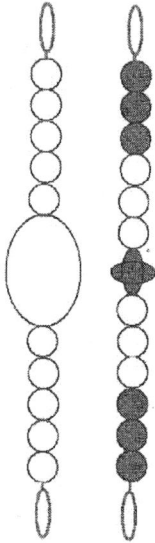

For the pattern of the first hanging row, I have decided to use a simple one. I have one bar on each end that is completely gold, while the other bars create a very simple pattern. The finished hanging row will look similar to the picture below, but we are not there yet. For now, you can just look at the picture to get an indication of what we are trying to achieve.

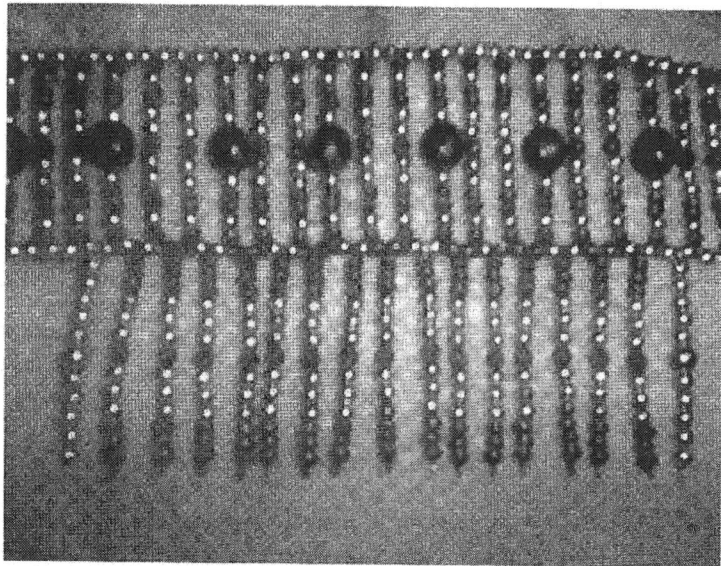

Once you have finished making the bars for the first hanging row, you will need to set them aside for a moment.

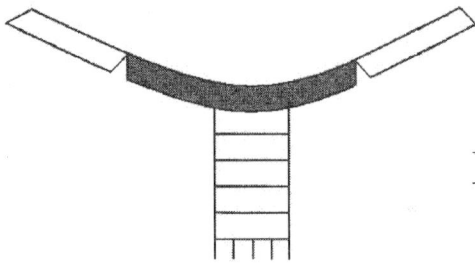

Egyptian Belt
Middle Segment

Now we will work on the middle segment. The first thing you should do is gather up your belt and establish where the very center of the middle segment is. I have taken an extra pin and twisted it to mark where the center of my middle segment is for future reference. From the center, you should be able to figure out where you will place the first hanging row. To do this, simply figure out where the center of the hanging row will be, and align it with the center of the middle segment.

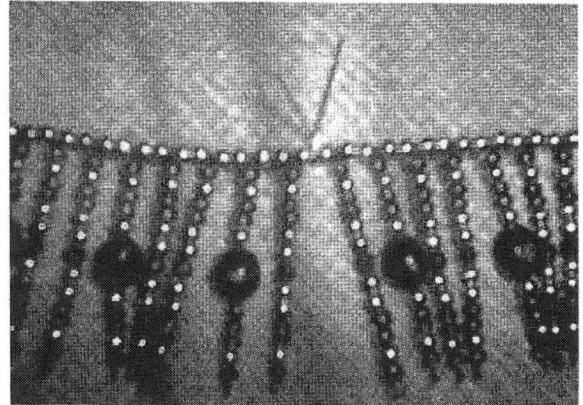

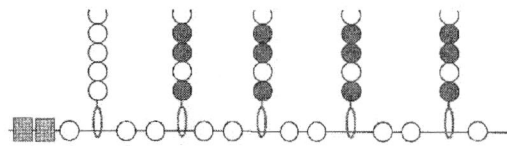

Once you have an idea of where the first hanging row will need to be placed, you can now start lacing the bottom of the middle segment together. You will begin this process the same way you laced together the side segments. Start by cutting your wire a few inches longer than the middle segment. Add two crimp beads to the end of the wire and crimp them in place. Now add one small gold bead, lace the wire through the first bar, add two gold beads, lace the string through the second bar, add two gold beads and continue on until you have reached the spot where you want your first hanging row to be placed.

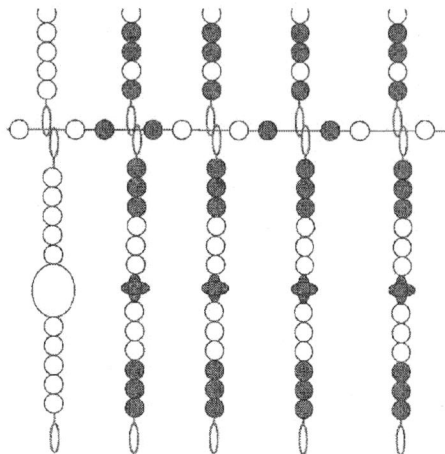

When you get to where the hanging row will be, you will lace it through the bottom of the middle segment, the same way you did on the rows of the necklace. The only difference is that instead of using two gold beads as spacers between the bars, we will change the pattern and use two red, then two gold, then two red, then two gold. This helps break up the straight gold line that would be present if we only used gold beads. Using all gold beads to lace the hanging rows will create a very noticeable gold line between the rows and is a tad distracting, and will make the belt look as though it is made of various rectangles. Changing the spacer bead pattern helps maintain the focus on the various bar patterns, instead of the spacer beads.

Once you have finished lacing the first hanging row to the bottom of the middle segment, your piece should look similar to the picture below.

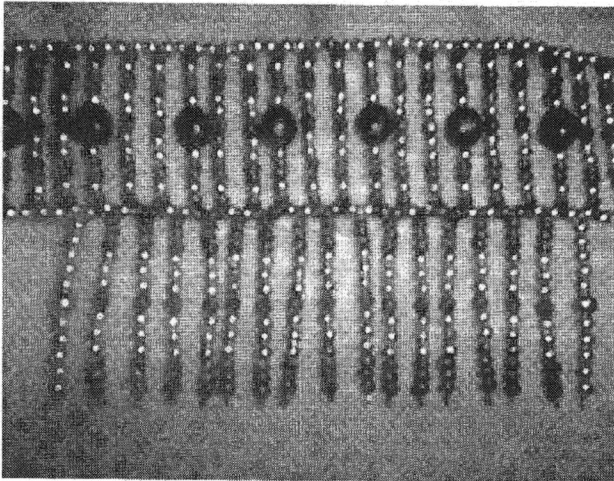

Now that you have the first hanging row attached, you can finish lacing up the rest of the middle segment, using two gold beads as spacers between the bars (the same way you laced up the side segments). When you've placed your last bar on the middle segment, add one small gold bead, then add two crimp beads and crimp them into place, leaving very little slack, only about ¼ of an inch.

You will be glad to know that the rest is smooth sailing from here on out! The rest of the hanging rows will be a breeze, and the other accessories to your outfit are very easy to make. You're almost done!

To help the rest of the rows come together smoothly, you will need to cut five pieces of thread about an inch or two longer than the length of the hanging rows. Place two crimp beads on the end of each individual string, and crimp them all in place. Set them aside for a moment and begin to prepare the bars for the remaining hanging rows.

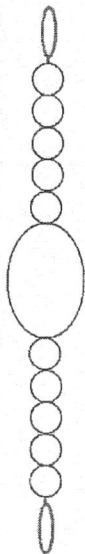

If you would like, you may go ahead and prepare the bars that will be paced at the beginning of each row, and at the end of each row. These will be bars with all gold beads. For six of the bars you will need to place five small gold beads at the top of the bar, one medium gold bead in the center, and five more small gold beads at the bottom.

Because one of our rows is a tiny bit longer than the other rows, you will need two bars that have two additional beads placed on them. For these two bars you will need to place six small gold beads at the top, one medium gold bead in the center and six more small gold beads. The two longer bars will be placed on the fourth row. I'll remind you later on as to when you will need them.

When you are done preparing all eight bars, you may set them aside and get to work on the rest of the main bars for each hanging row.

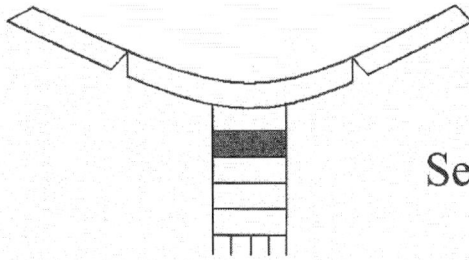

Egyptian Belt
Second Hanging Row

For the second row, we will be using two bar patterns as seen below, plus the two gold bars that will be placed on the end. If you are using 17 bars to create each of your rows, then you will need 8 bars of one pattern, and 7 bars of the other pattern.

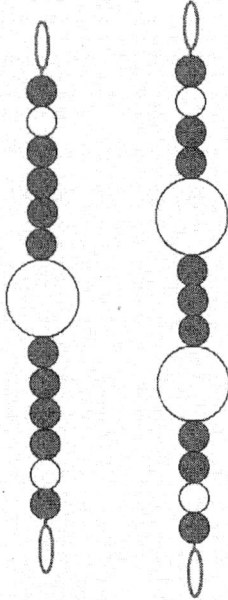

Once you have your bars completed, gather up your wire (one of the ones that you made earlier and have already added the crimp beads to), and add one small gold bead to the wire, then add one gold beaded bar, then lace it through the bottom of the first bar from the row above. Now, lace the two rows together, exactly the way you attached the first hanging row to the middle segment, by alternating the spacer beads as red and gold.

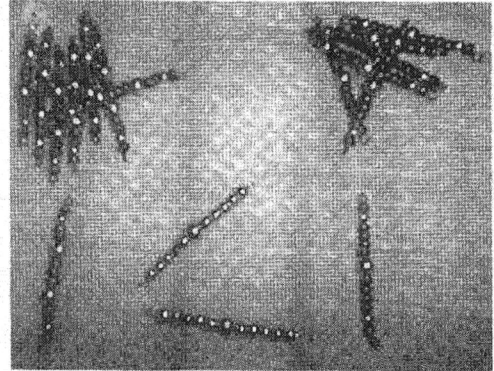

When you have added your last bar, then add one gold bead and two crimp beads. Leave about ¼ of an inch slack and then crimp the crimp beads into place. Cut off the excess wire.

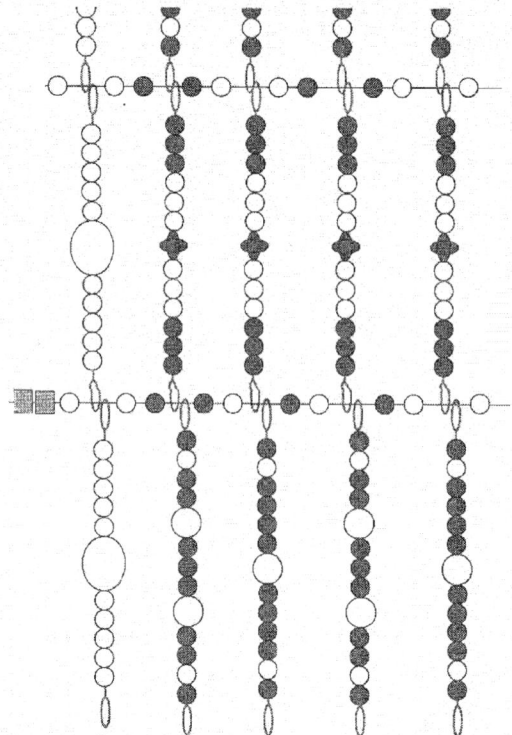

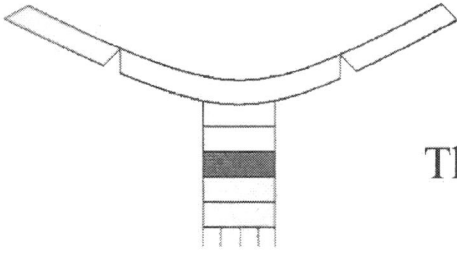

Egyptian Belt
Third Hanging Row

For the third row, we will be using two bar patterns as seen below, plus the two gold bars that will be placed on the end. If you are using 17 bars to create each of your rows, then you will need 8 bars of one pattern, and 7 bars of the other pattern.

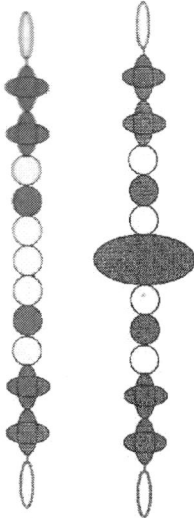

Once you have your bars completed, gather up your wire (one of the ones that you made earlier and have already added the crimp beads to), and add one small gold bead to the wire, then add one gold beaded bar, then lace it through the bottom of the first bar from the row above. Now, lace the two rows together, exactly the way you did before. Remember to add one gold bead to the end, then crimp your two crimp beads in place and cut off the excess wire.

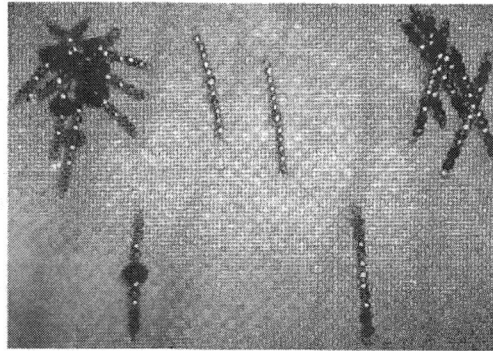

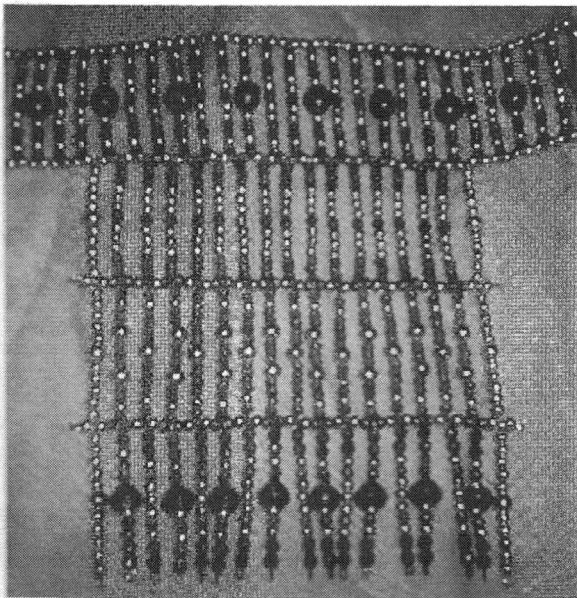

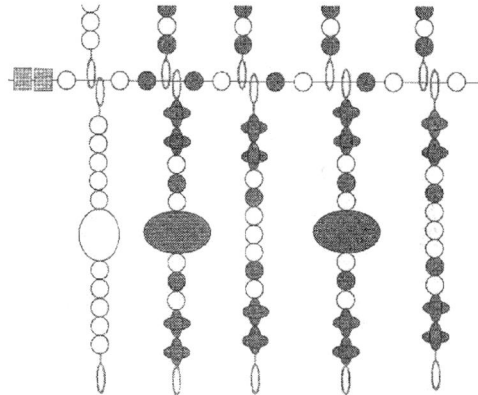

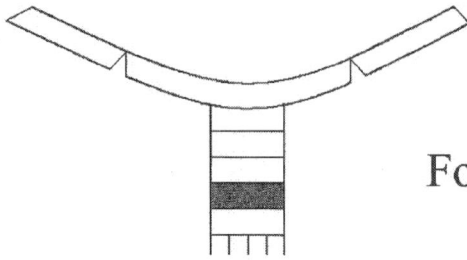

Egyptian Belt
Fourth Hanging Row

For the fourth row, we will be using two bar patterns as seen below, plus the two gold bars that will be placed on the end (we will be using the 2 longer gold bars on this row). If you are using 17 bars to create each of your rows, then you will need 8 bars of one pattern, and 7 bars of the other pattern.

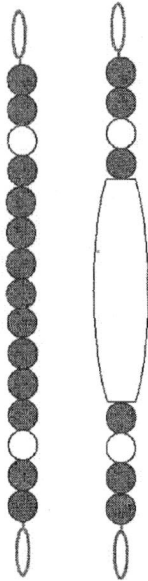

Once you have your bars completed, gather up your wire (one of the ones that you made earlier and have already added the crimp beads to), and add one small gold bead to the wire, then add one gold beaded bar, then lace it through the bottom of the first bar from the row above. Now, lace the two rows together, exactly the way you did before. Remember to add one gold bead to the end, then crimp the two crimp beads in place and cut off the excess wire.

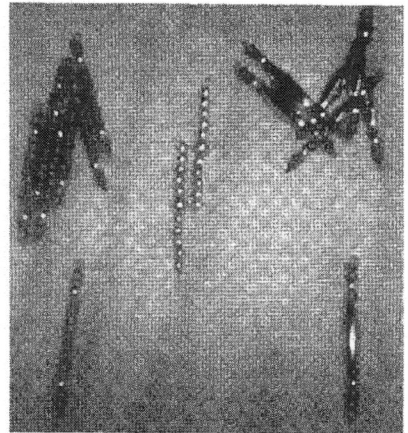

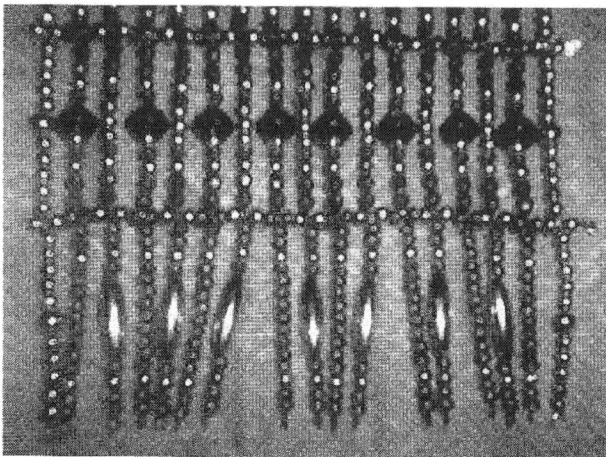

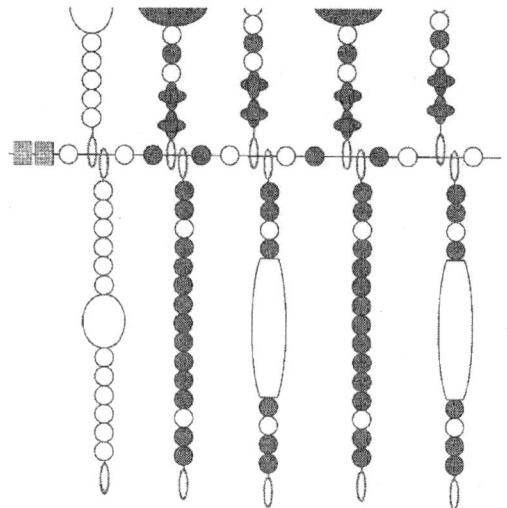

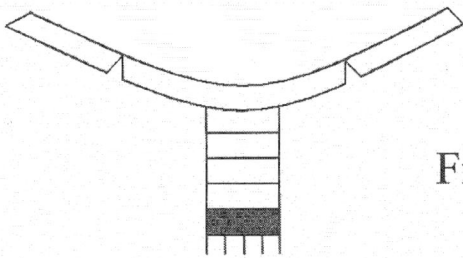

Egyptian Belt
Fifth Hanging Row

For the fifth row, we will be using two bar patterns as seen below, plus the two gold bars that will be placed on the end. If you are using 17 bars to create each of your rows, then you will need 5 bars of one pattern, and 10 bars of the other pattern.

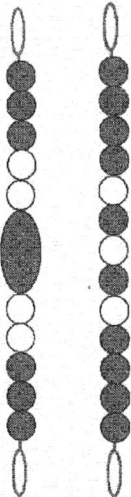

Once you have your bars completed, gather up your wire (one of the ones that you made earlier and have already added the crimp beads to), and add one small gold bead to the wire, then add one gold beaded bar, then lace it through the bottom of the first bar from the row above. Now, lace the two rows together, exactly the way you did before. You can use the picture below as reference on how to place the bars to get the two patterns placed evenly. Remember to add one gold bead to the end, then crimp the crimp beads in place and cut off the excess wire.

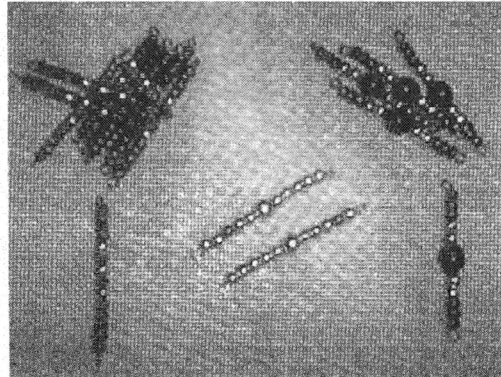

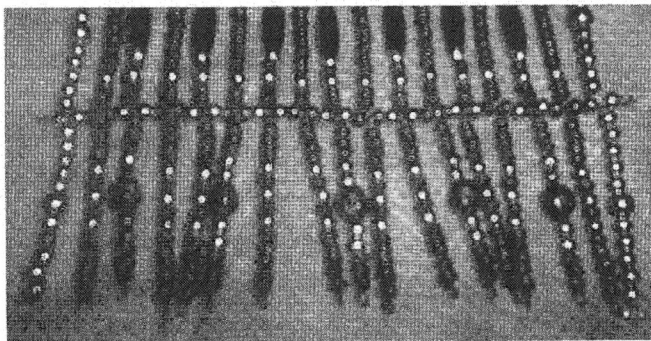

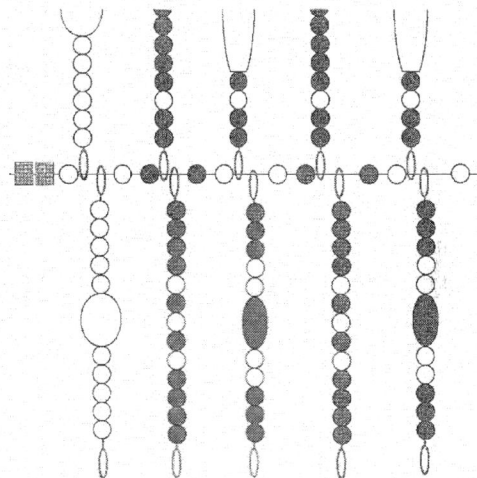

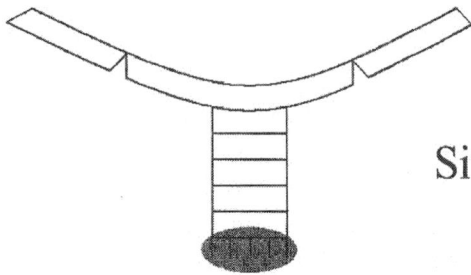

Egyptian Belt
Sixth Dangling Row

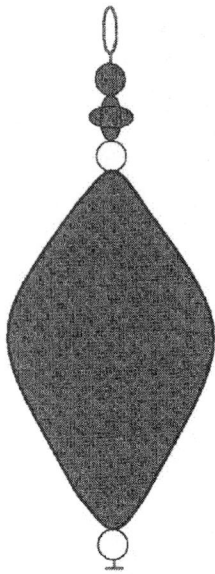

For the sixth row, we will be using one pattern as seen below. These bars should be made with flat head pins instead of eye pins. Once you have your bars completed, gather up your last wire (of the ones that you made earlier and have already added the crimp beads to), and add one small gold bead, then add one gold beaded bar, then lace it through the bottom of the first bar from the row above. Now, lace the two rows together, exactly the way you did before, except with the new bars, you will only be adding them to every 5th bar on the row, as shown in the picture.

To make it look evenly spaced you can add the bars between the spacer beads, which is how they are placed in the illustration below. This time, if you want to use all gold beads as the spacers between the bars, you can. This is the very bottom of the belt, so a gold line will not look out of place. When you are done lacing the bars together, remember to add one gold bead to the end of the wire, then crimp the two crimp beads in place and cut off the excess wire.

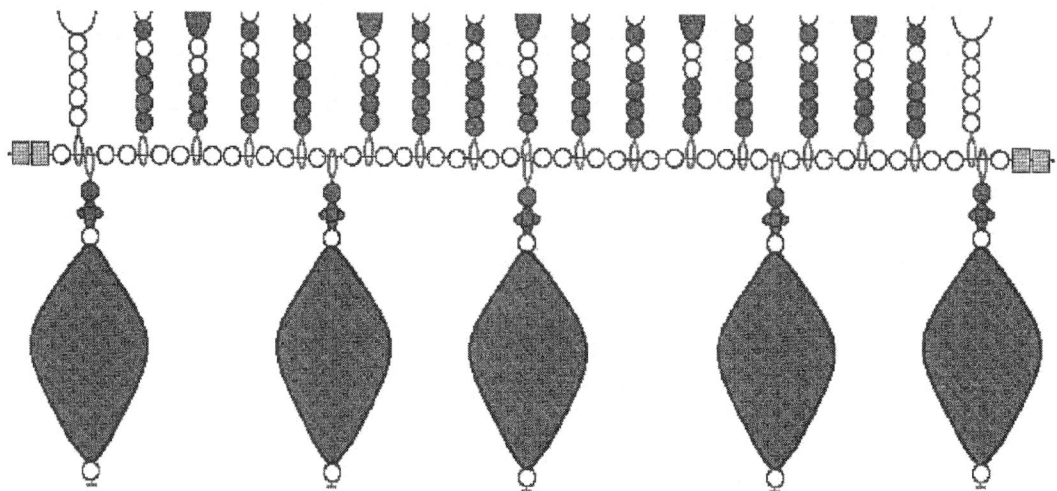

When you have completed the bottom row of the belt, your belt will be completely finished! It should look similar to the one in the picture below, but it might look even better!

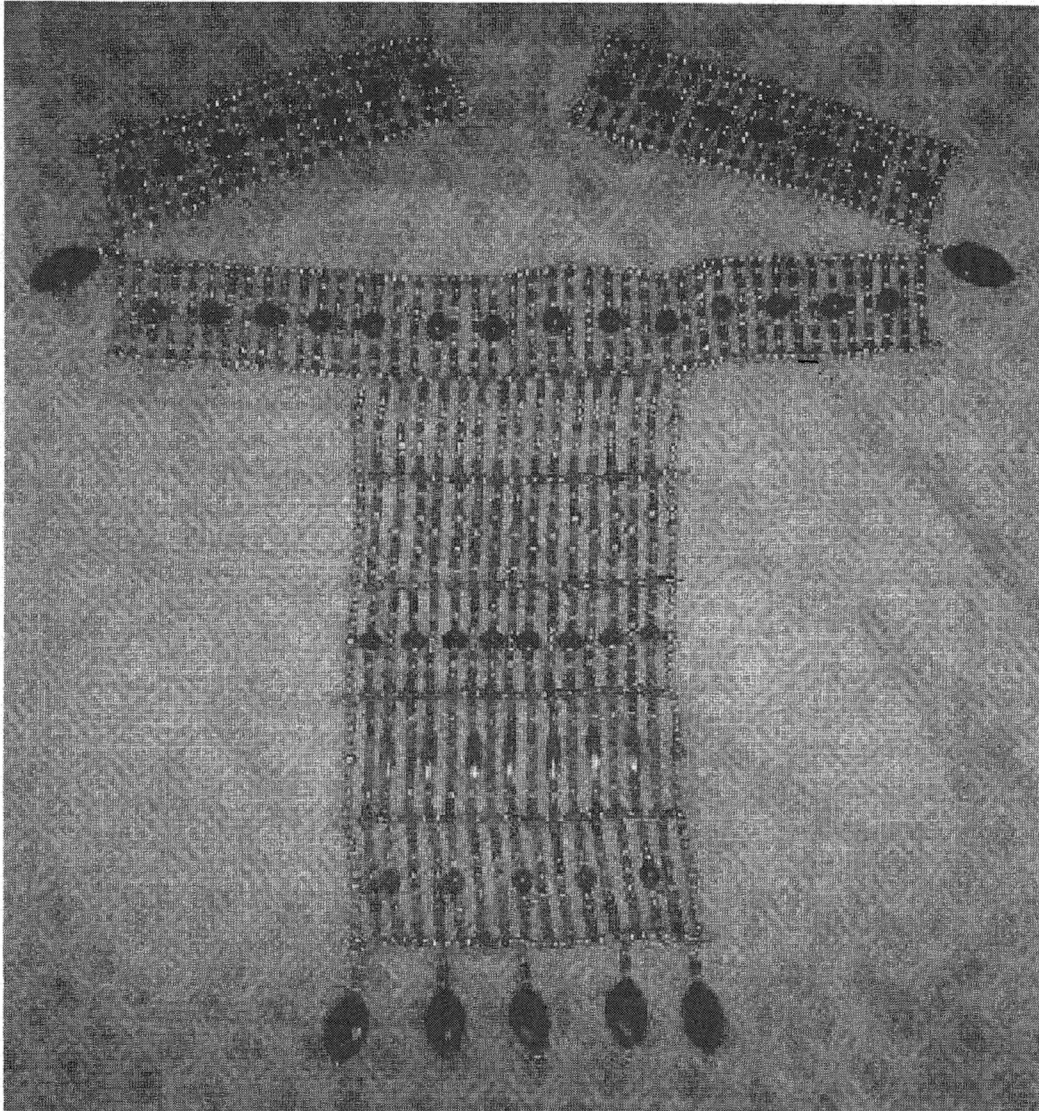

EGYPTIAN INSPIRED
ACCESSORIES
EARRINGS, BRACELETS, ARMBANDS, & ANKLETS

Earrings to Match your
Egyptian Collar Necklace

The earrings are by far the easiest pieces of jewelry to make within this set, so after completing the necklace and belt, you might be ready for a quick and easy project. For the earrings, you will need two flat head pins, and two fish hook earrings. (If you don't have two fish hook earrings, you can make your own using two eye pins. Just take the two eye pins and shape them with your pliers, making sure that the looped end remains at the bottom of the pieces, as shown in the pattern above.)

Take the flat head pins and slide on to each: a small gold bead, a small red bead, a medium gold bead, a larger red bead, a medium gold bead, a small red bead, and finally, another small gold bead, as illustrated in the pattern above.

When you are finished applying the beads to the bars, make sure that there is not too much extra bare bar on the end. If there is, you will need to cut off the excess bar, leaving only enough to make your loop at the top.

When you have the bar length right, make your loop, making sure to leave it slightly open. Place the loop from the bottom of the fish hook into the slightly opened loop of your bar. Now close the loop on the bar. You're done!

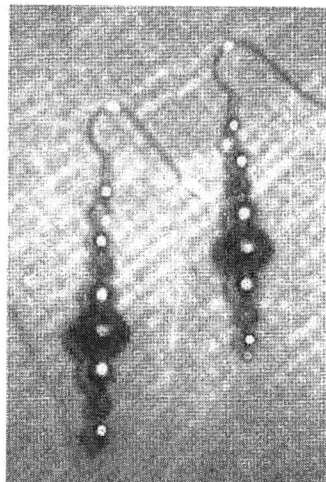

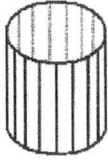

Bracelets
To Match Your Egyptian Garb

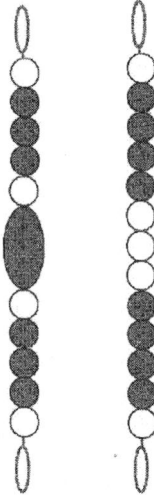

For the bracelets, you will need to measure your wrists to see how much cord you will need. You will need two cords for each bracelet; one to lace the top of the bars, and one to lace the bottom of the bars, for a total of four pieces of cord to create two bracelets. Use the illustration in the upper right-hand corner to see where along your wrist you should measure for the cord.

On each cord, give yourself about two inches extra cord to make it easier to work with. I also recommend highly that you use elastic cord, and measure your wrists for a firm fit so that the pieces do not slide up and down your wrist as you wear them. The bars will create a heavy piece of jewelry, so the piece will need to fit firmly.

NOTE: The number of spacer beads you use between each bar can vary. In my pattern, I show two small gold beads placed between each bar, which creates a more substantial pattern; however, if you would like the bars farther apart, for an airier feel, you can use three or four beads. If you would like your bars to be as close as possible, you can just use one spacer bead. I have found that two or three beads works best, particularly when I use larger beads on the bars, as two or three spacer beads will allow room for the larger beads to rest nicely on the bars without bumping into the other large beads. In the picture, I illustrate using two spacer beads. In the photos, I use three spacer beads. You can look at both, or even dabble with both and see what works best for you. You can also make this judgment on the remaining armbands and anklets. The only thing to bear in mind is, it will look better if all of the pieces match, and you use the same amount of spacer beads between the bars on each accessory.

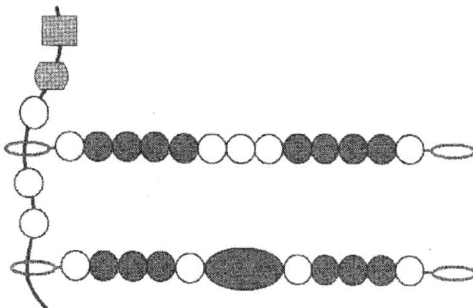

The bars we will use to create the bracelet will consist of two bar patterns, as seen above. To begin the bracelets, attach one crimp bead and clamp it into place on the very end of the cord. Now, add one extra crimp bead, but do not crimp it yet. Add one small gold bead, and then add your first bar. Add two (or three) small gold beads, and then your second bar. Repeat the process until you have reached your desired length.

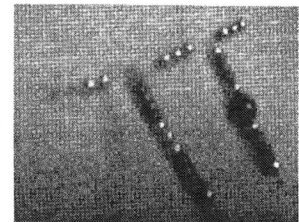

44

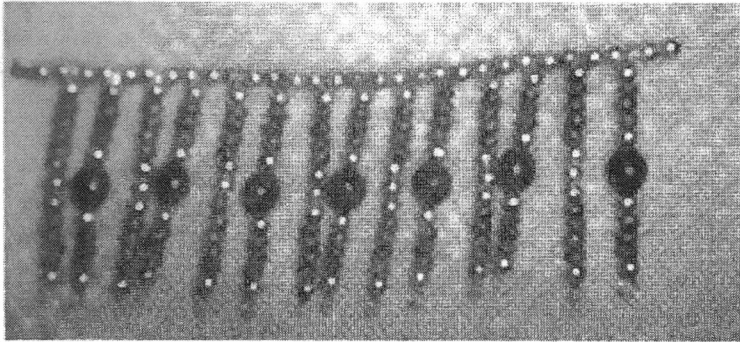

To make sure the length is accurate you can test it by wrapping it around your wrist before finishing the strand off.

Once you have your desired length, lace the end of the cord through the loose crimp bead, as shown in the illustration below.

Now, tighten the strand so that all of the beads and bars come together nice and snug. Then, crimp down the crimp bead. You can now cut off the excess cord and the first crimp bead that you used to start the strand, as seen below.

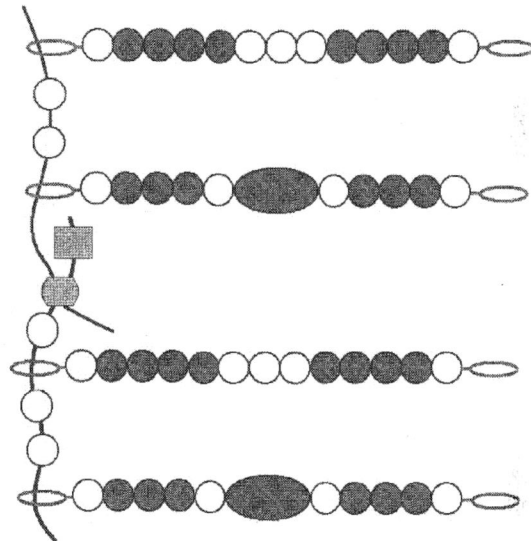

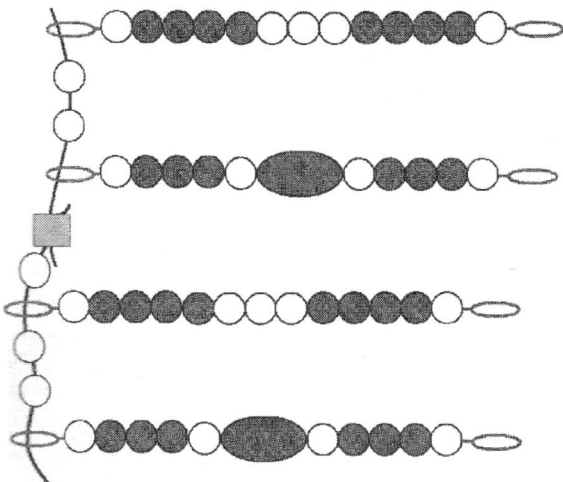

Once you have the first row completed, it should look similar to the strand below.

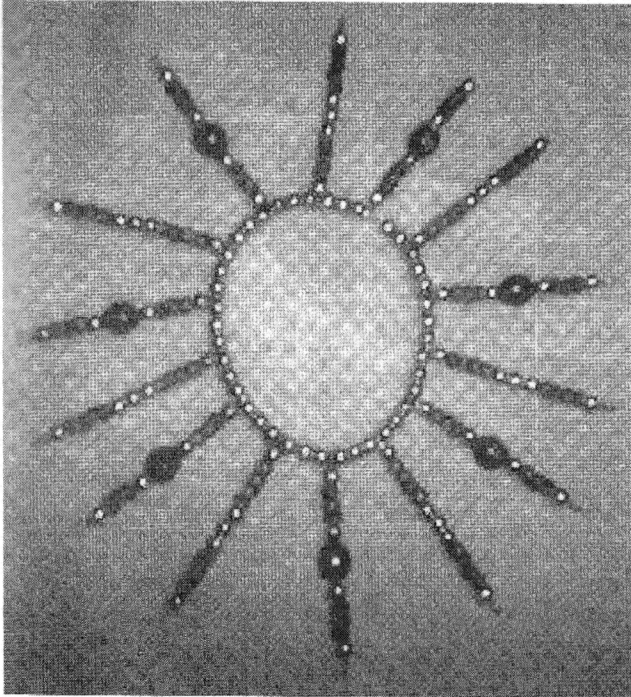

You can now lace together the bottom. You will perform the exact same procedure for lacing the bottom that you previously performed for the top.

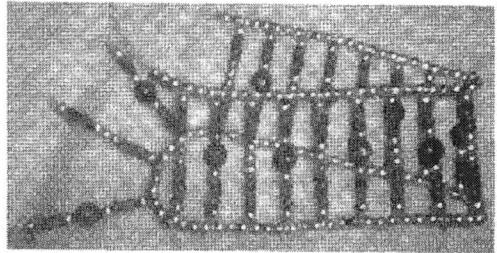

When you have competed lacing together the bottom of your bars, the bracelets will be completely finished, and should look similar to the picture below.

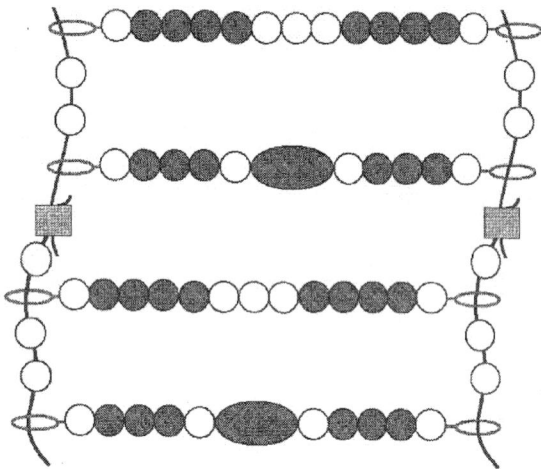

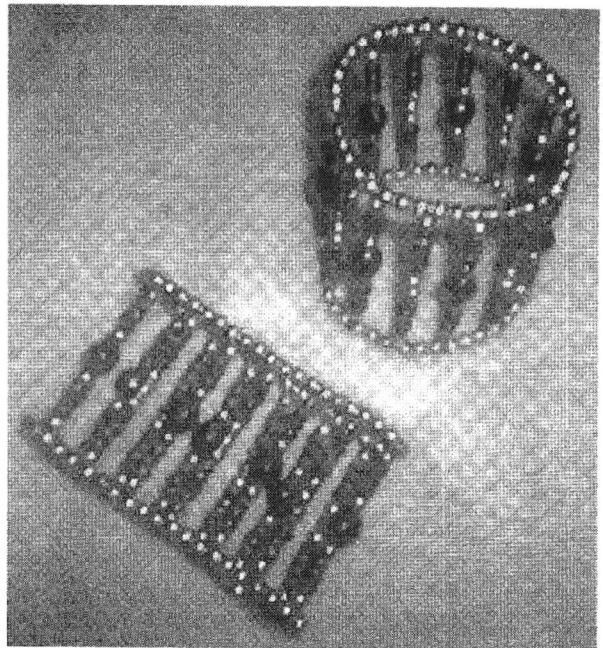

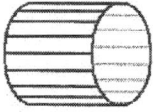

Armbands
To Match Your Egyptian Garb

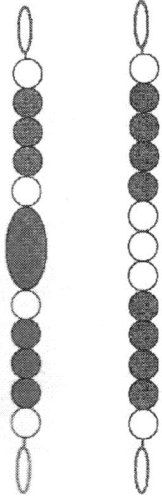

For the Arm Bands, you will be do exactly the same thing you did to create the bracelets, except you may be adding a few more bars, depending on the size of your upper arm.

You will need to measure your upper arm to see how much cord you will need. You will need two cords for each armband; one to lace the top of the bars, and one to lace the bottom of the bars, for a total of four pieces of cord to create two arm bands. Use the illustration in the upper right-hand corner to see where along your arm that you should measure for the cord.

On each cord, give yourself about two inches extra cord to make it easier to work with. I also highly recommend that you use elastic cord, and measure your arms for a firm fit so that the pieces do not slide down your arm as you wear them. The bars will create a heavy piece of jewelry, so the piece will need to fit firmly.

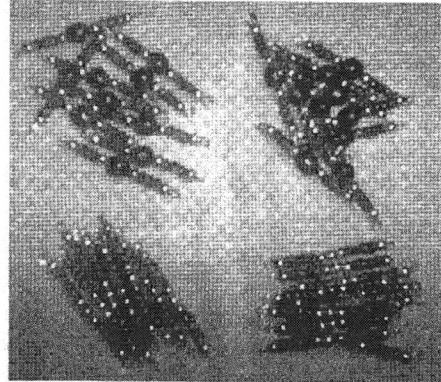

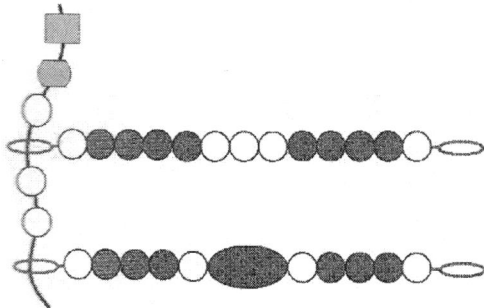

The bars we will use to create the armband are the same as the bracelet, and will once again consist of two bar patterns, as seen above. To begin the armbands, attach one crimp

bead and clamp it into place on the end of one of the cords. Now, add one extra crimp bead, but do not crimp it yet. Add one small gold bead, and then add your first bar. Add two small gold beads, and then your second bar. Repeat the process until you have reached your desired length. To make sure the length is accurate you can test it by wrapping it around your upper arm before finishing the strand off. Once you have your desired length, lace the end of the cord through the loose crimp bead, as shown in the illustration.

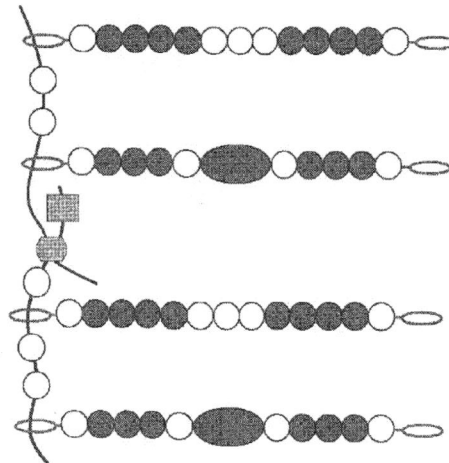

47

Now, tighten the strand so that all of the beads and bars come together nice and snug. Then, crimp down the crimp bead. You can now cut off the excess cord and the first crimp bead that you used to start the strand, as seen below.

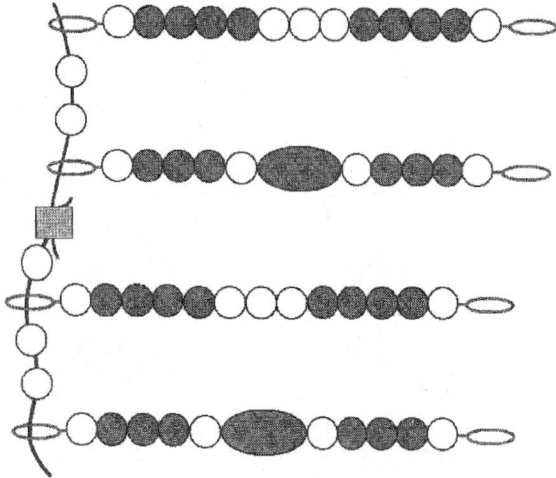

Once you have completed the first strand, you can now lace together the bottom. You will perform the exact same procedure for lacing the bottom that you previously performed for the top.

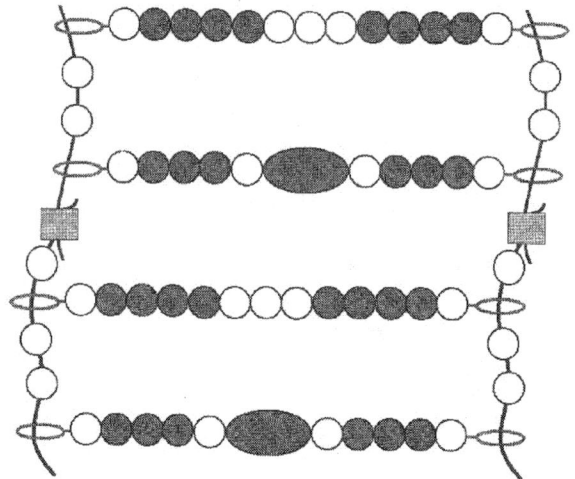

When you have competed lacing together the bottom of your bars, the armbands will be completely finished, and should look similar to the picture below.

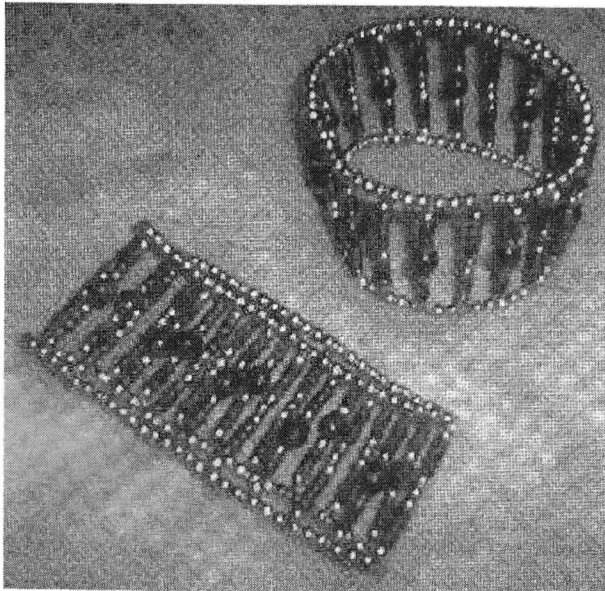

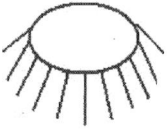

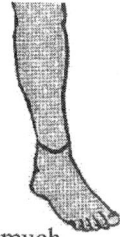

Anklets
To Match Your Egyptian Garb

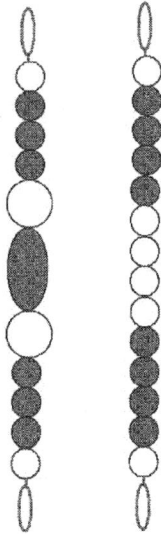

For the anklets, you will need to measure your ankle to see how much cord you will need. You will only need one cord for each anklet, for lacing the top of the bars, for a total of two pieces of cord to create two anklets. Use the illustration in the upper right-hand corner to see where along your ankle you should measure for the cord.

On each cord, give yourself about two inches extra cord to make it easier to work with. Once again, I also recommend highly that you use elastic cord, and measure your ankles for a firm fit so that the pieces do not slide off down the back of your heal as you wear them. The bars will create a heavy piece of jewelry, so the piece will need to fit firmly.

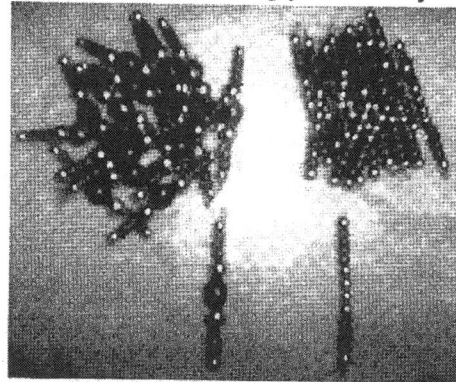

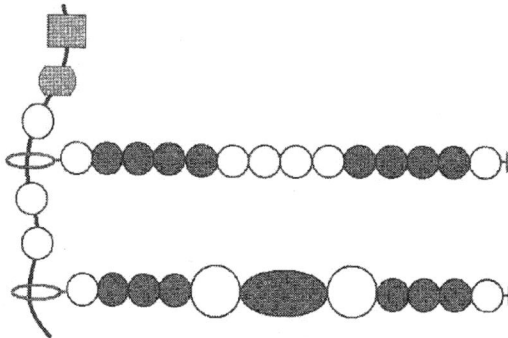

The bars we will use to create the anklet are the slightly different from the bars we used to create the armbands and bracelets, as I used two larger gold beads on these bars, instead of the small ones. The bars will again, consist of two bar patterns, as seen above. To begin the anklets, attach one crimp bead to the end of the cord and clamp it into place.

Now, add one extra crimp bead, but do not crimp it yet. Add one small gold bead, and then add your first bar. Add two small gold beads, and then your second bar. Repeat the process until you have reached your desired length. To make sure the length is accurate you can test it by wrapping it around your ankle before finishing the strand off.

Once you have your desired length, lace the end of the cord through the loose crimp bead, as shown in the illustration on the right.

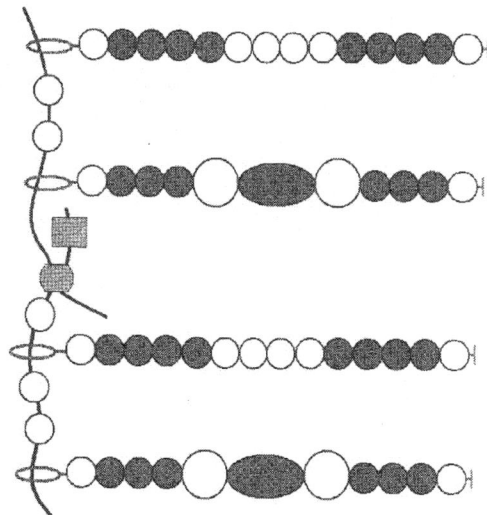

Now, tighten the strand so that all of the beads and bars come together nice and snug. Then, crimp down the crimp bead. You can now cut off the excess cord and the first crimp bead that you used to start the strand, as seen below.

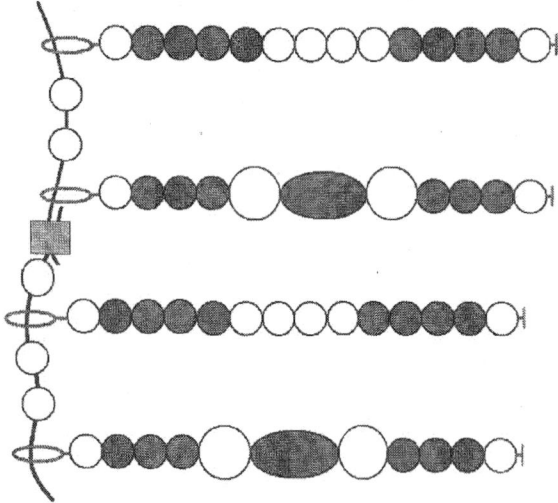

When you have competed lacing together the top of your bars, the anklets will be completely finished, and should look similar to the pictures below.

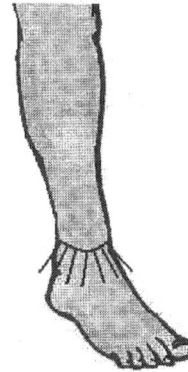

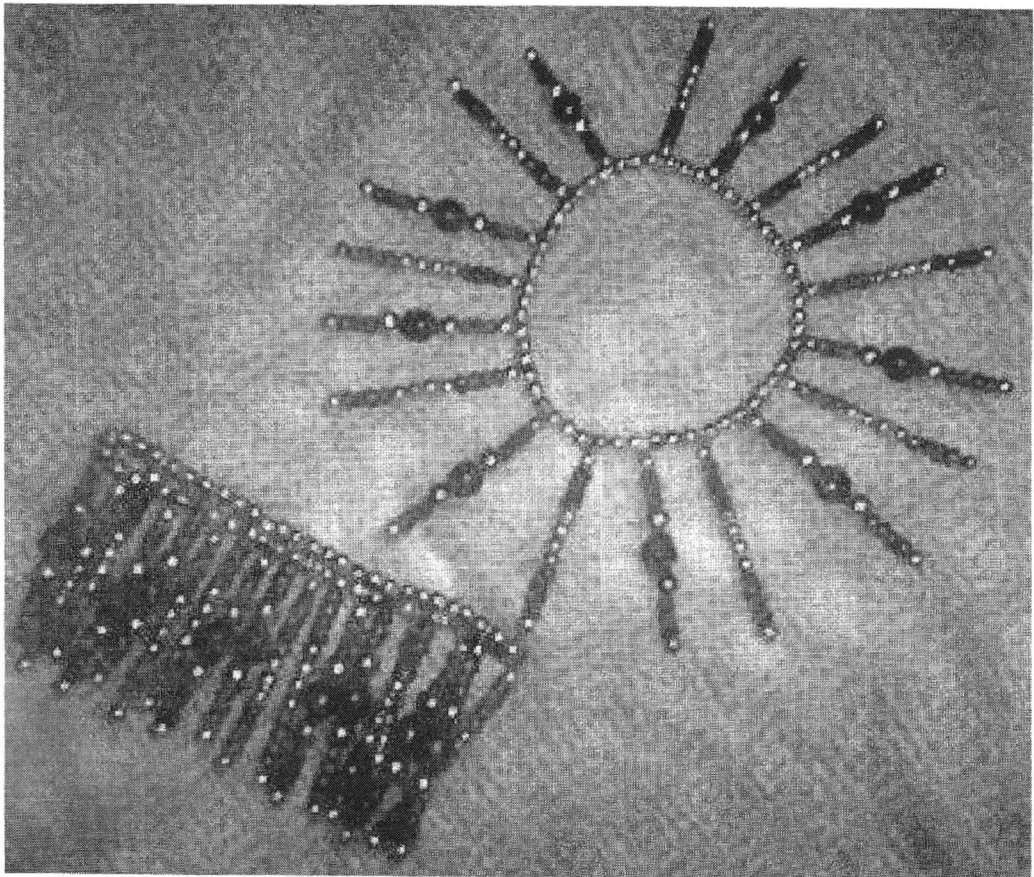

OTHER EGYPTIAN INSPIRED
DESIGNS

The necklace below (enlarged on the right) was produced using gold and black beads. A color photo is visible on the back cover. The first two rows are made of 2-inch bars, while the third row is comprised of 1-inch bars.

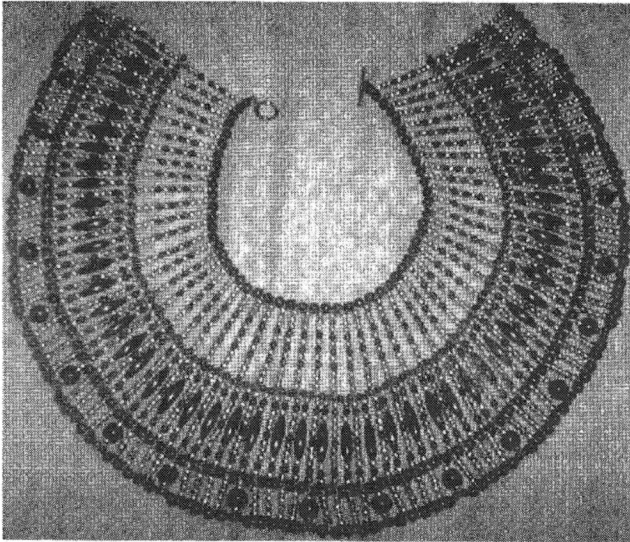

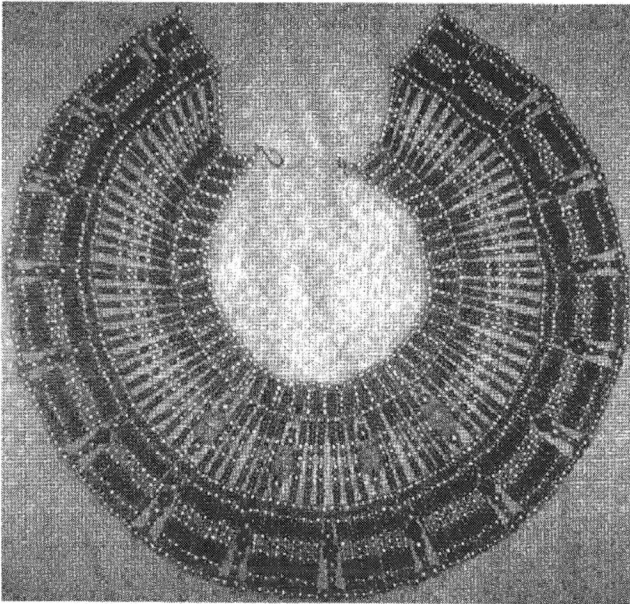

The necklace above (enlarged on the right) was produced using dark green, gold and scarab beads. A color photo is visible on the back cover. The first row is made of 1-inch bars, while the second and third rows are comprised of 2-inch bars.

The necklace below (enlarged on the right) was produced using peach, beige-iridescent, gold and various brown toned beads. A color photo is visible on the back cover. All three rows were produced using 2-inch bars.

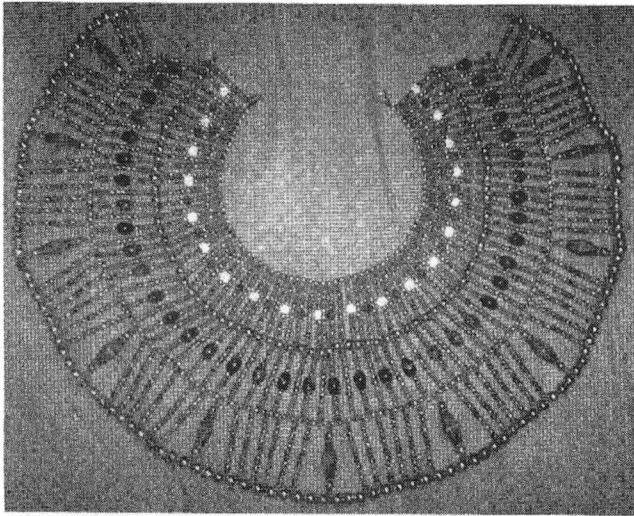

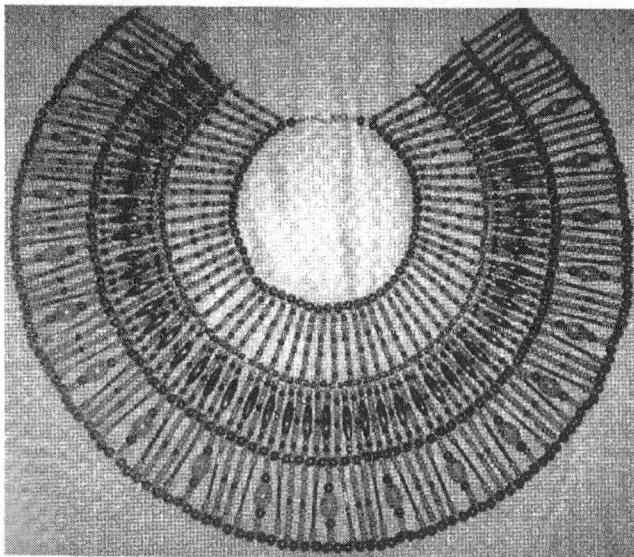

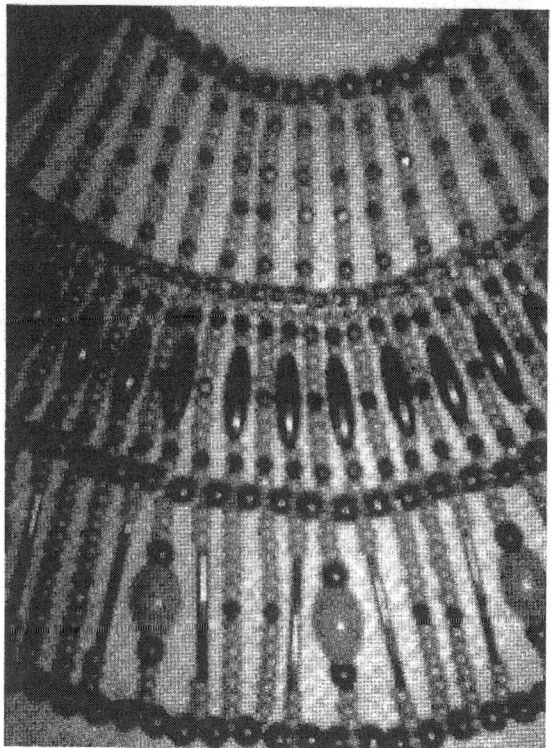

The necklace above (enlarged on the right) was produced using black and red beads. A color photo is visible on the back cover. All three rows were produced using 2-inch bars.

Other Books by Dawna Flowers

www. Dawna Flowers .com

Fiction

In the Forest, Horror Novella
Sea Loot, Horror Novel
Neighbors, Horror Novel (Coming Soon)

Children Fiction Titles

Deep in the Forest
Along Came Cthulhu
Story of Krampus
Bigfoot of the Big Woods
The Crazy 'Coon Lady
Deeper in the Forest
Helpful Hank
Sally Scratch & the Squirrel
The Bat House Bag
Wolves of Woodsmen County

Non-Fiction

Help with Hauntings
The Book of Dark & Light Shadows
The Spell Book of Wiccan Shadows
Witch Wars
The Wiccan Holiday Cookbook
Book of Cleansings: Professionals Prayer Collection

www.Peculiar Packages.com

Printed in Great Britain
by Amazon